Supplementary Volume no. 9

PLATO'S ARGUMENTS FOR FORMS

by

ROBERT WILLIAM JORDAN

Fellow of St John's College, Cambridge

THE CAMBRIDGE PHILOLOGICAL SOCIETY

1983

ISBN 0 906014 05 0

Printed in Great Britain by the University Press, Cambridge

CONTENTS

INTRODUCTION

No philosophical theory fools all the people all of the time (that, perhaps, lies in the nature of philosophical theories as such); and the theory of Forms – criticized and modified by Plato himself in his later works, and further modified or abandoned by his immediate successors – has perhaps found less adherents than most philosophical theories. And yet it retains its interest today, and will doubtless continue to do so.

In the chapters that follow, I try to establish certain historical claims about the nature of the theory and the nature of the problems it was designed to meet. I do not attempt to say *why* I think Plato faced these problems, nor yet what makes the theory of Forms so deep and interesting. I hope, nonetheless, that my work may serve as a first step towards answering these more important questions, by showing clearly *what* the course of some of Plato's own thought about Forms actually was.

The two most widely believed accounts of the theory of Forms are perhaps those of Vlastos and Owen. Vlastos, on the one hand, holds that Plato is trying to make a distinction between two different sorts of proposition, the contingent (examplified in the sensible world) and the logically necessary (exemplified in Forms). Owen, on the other hand, believes that Plato to some extent misunderstood the logic of his language, and that the theory of Forms represents a mistaken attempt to make all words behave in the same way – to make 'incomplete' predicates behave like 'complete' ones.

Both these two accounts of the theory of Forms are perhaps, in their different ways, too strongly coloured by our knowledge of the subsequent development of philosophy. Thus Wittgenstein lies behind Owen's view of Plato, and Kant behind Vlastos'. Certainly, I hope to show by detailed examination of Plato's texts, that neither of these two different views of the theory of Forms gives the most persuasive account of those passages in which Plato explains why he thinks we should adopt this theory.

The account I shall offer of the theory of Forms proposes that Plato was deeply troubled by an issue concerning the nature of real and apparent contradiction that does not concern us at all nowadays, but that did interest Plato's predecessors Parmenides and Heraclitus. I shall contend that Plato returns time and again to the contemplation of some x that is F in relation to y, but is not F in relation to z, and that he does so because he does not fully understand how to characterize such states of affairs. He can see, as we can all see, that such states of affairs occur, and so are possible, and are not contradictory. But, unlike us, Plato feels the need to pose the further question 'but *how* is it that such states of affairs are possible?'; 'how *can* there be some x that is F in relation to y but is not F in relation of z?'. I shall contend that the form taken by the theory of Forms in Plato's middle period is largely dictated by Plato's need to answer this question.

Acknowledgements: this work constitutes a revision of a Cambridge doctoral dissertation submitted in May 1980. The topic was originally suggested to me by G. E. L. Owen, who also supervised the first year of my graduate work. Drafts of the complete thesis were read by Margaret Pedler and Melanie Johnson. Both saved me from many errors. Prof. J. L. Ackrill and Myles Burnyeat made many accurate criticisms of the work at my thesis examination. Myles Burnyeat made further numerous accute criticisms of the final draft of this revision of the work. I owe the greatest debt, however, to Malcolm Schofield, who supervised the greater part of my work on the original thesis. Without his sound philosophical judgement, and shrewd character assessment, the ideas expressed here would never have found appropriate form.

I would further like to thank the Faculty of Classics of the University of Cambridge, and the Master and Fellows of St John's College, Cambridge, for their generous financial assistance which has made possible the publication of this work in this form.

1. RECOLLECTION, ETHICS, DEFINITION AND THE THEORY OF FORMS

Introduction

In chapters 2-4 of this work, I hope to provide at least a partial answer to the question 'why did Plato have a theory of Forms?', and to do so, by considering a number of arguments with which, I believe, Plato presents us, in favour of the theory of Forms.

In this chapter, by contrast, I propose to compare my own approach to this question, with that implied by another, very widely held belief about the theory of Forms – that Plato simply assumes the truth of the theory, and presents no arguments in favour of it.[1] I hope to show not only what the difficulties are with the view that Plato assumed the theory of Forms without argument, but also, in the process, to show as clearly as possible how we should understand the question 'why does Plato have a theory of Forms?' (for before we can set about answering this question, we must decide what it means).

I do not propose to discuss *all* the various reasons that commentators have suggested might have motivated Plato to assume the theory of Forms without argument. Some of the suggestions made I do not discuss here because they are clearly mistaken: for instance, I do not discuss the view that Plato was concerned about the necessary imperfection of all sensible representations of geometrical figures, and so on. As Crombie has shown, there is no evidence in the text of Plato to support this view[2] – though it is a view that certainly has been canvassed.[3] Then again, I do not discuss the view held by Vlastos among others, that a religious mysticism was one of Plato's reasons for holding the theory of Forms.[4] For in so far as this view is right, the theory of Forms is not liable to philosophical discussion and criticism, and so we cannot answer the question why Plato had a theory of Forms in philosophical terms. And I, in common with other commentators, am concerned to make philosophical sense of the theory of Forms. Finally, it should be noted that commentators have sometimes set down Plato's assumptions about knowledge and explanation as reasons for assuming the theory of Forms without argument;[5] and that I do not discuss these views here, but take them up in chapters 3 and 4. The views about the theory of Forms that I do propose to discuss here share two characteristics: *prima facie* they all seem quite plausible answers to the question 'why did Plato have a theory of Forms?', but, on closer examination, they all prove inadequate.

Now the reasons commentators suggest as to why Plato might have assumed the theory of Forms without argument vary in accordance with the general view they take of the development of Plato's thought. A commentator might choose to stress the continuity in Plato's thinking between the early period and the middle period. And if a commentator takes *this* line about the development of Plato's thought, he is likely to see in the theory a new (or possibly, as we shall see, the same old) solution to the problems set by the Socratic question and by relativism in ethics.[6] Alternatively, a commentator might choose to emphasize that there are a number of new and related ideas in Plato's middle period thought, and to maintain that we cannot hope to understand the theory of Forms, unless we see it in the light of the revolution in Plato's thought. And of course it is also possible to combine elements from these two views about the development of Plato's thought, and see the theory both in relation to the problems of the early dialogues, and in relation to the new doctrines of the middle period.

Now of course there is some truth in both these two divergent accounts of the development of Plato's thought. But neither of them, I believe, helps us to understand by Plato had a theory of Forms (given the interpretation of this question that I shall argue for). I shall turn first to Plato's theory of recollection, and argue that it illustrates very well both what it sound in these two views about the development of Plato's thought, and also their inadequacy where the theory of Forms is concerned.

Forms and Recollection

I shall deal first with the theory of recollection as it is expressed in the *Phaedo*. The recollection doctrine here involves several of the new claims Plato makes in the middle period – that body and soul must be distinguished, that there are Forms, that these Forms can be known by the soul whereas the sensible world is known (or possibly believed) by the senses; and the recollection doctrine further insists that Forms are known by the soul before birth.

Now the first point I want to make about the passage in question here, is that it does not present us with a formal argument for the theory of Forms. I do not wish to deny that Plato's epistemological views did lead him to posit Forms. In fact, it seems to me that we do find Plato basing an argument for the theory of Forms on epistemological considerations in the *Timaeus* and in *Republic V*; *that* argument is the subject of my chapter 3. When I discuss the argument there, it will become clear that it does not involve any essential reference to the dichotomy between body and soul (or, *a fortiori*, to the theory of recollection). Here I aim to show that the argument in *Phaedo* 72ff. gives us no independent reason for maintaining the theory of Forms.

The argument in 72e-73a is introduced as an exposition of Socrates' theory of recollection. The argument for the theory of recollection involves an argument that the soul exists before birth. It does not involve an argument for the theory of Forms – though it *does* involve Plato in attempting to prove a number of propositions about Forms, such as that they are different from particulars, that they are known by the soul before birth, and are then (at birth) forgotten, and later recollected. But it is just assumed that Forms exist, when Simmias answers Socrates' question φαμέν πού τι εἶναι ... αὐτὸ τὸ ἴσον; at 74b1 in the affirmative: φῶμεν μέντοι νὴ Δία. So while I would by no means want to claim that we do not learn anything about Plato's conception of Forms from this passage (I discuss what I think we should make of it in chapter 5), it clearly cannot be regarded as a formal argument for the theory of Forms.[7]

But the real question here is not, of course, whether or not we find here a formal argument for the theory of Forms, but rather, whether this passage gives us any reason to think that Plato would still have maintained anything recognizable as the theory of Forms, had he not advanced formal arguments for the theory elsewhere.

It might seem that this is indeed the case. After all, the assumption that Forms exist is crucial to the argument for the theory of recollection presented in the passage. For if Forms do not exist, then it cannot be the case that they are different from particulars, and it cannot be the case that they are first known, then forgotten, and finally recollected. It might seem, then, that one reason why Plato believed in the theory of Forms was that he believed in the theory of recollection, and that the theory of Forms is a necessary constituent of the theory of recollection. (Let us suppose, for the moment, that Plato has reasons for holding the theory of recollection that are independent of his reasons for holding the theory of Forms, and that he argues for the theory of recollection without assuming the theory of Forms.)

So let us ascribe the following line of reasoning to Plato (so far as I can see, it is not one that he actually expresses anywhere): 'there must be Forms, because there must be entities recollected'. I propose to call this line of reasoning 'the argument from recollection' (it must not, of course, be confused with the argument *for* the theory of recollection).

Now the argument from recollection does not, I think, help us to answer the question that really interests us – why Plato had a theory of Forms. For this argument does not provide us with any grounds for ascribing to Forms any one of the characteristics which they are commonly said to possess.

It is worth elaborating on this point, and trying to formulate it as clearly as possible, as it is of the utmost theoretical importance. Forms, as we know them, have a number of properties that distinguish them from other classes of entity – and in particular, that distinguish them from sensible particulars. Forms exist forever, pure, unmixed, unchanging, incomposite, 'in every way being', 'in themselves', and stand in relation to particulars as does a model to copies to it.[8] Now not all these characteristics of Forms, perhaps, are essential properties of Forms; but when we ask why Plato had a theory of Forms, we are asking, as I see it, why Plato believed in entities to which he ascribes this particular set of characteristics, or at least, the most important of these characteristics.[9] And my point is that the argument from recollection that I have assembled on Plato's behalf, does not help us to see why Plato had a theory of Forms, if we do mean by that, why Plato had a theory of entities that exist forever, pure, unmixed, incomposite, and so on.

Now it is necessary, of course, given the conditions laid down for recollection in the *Phaedo*, that the objects that Plato there claims to be recollected are nonidentical with particulars. And because Plato assumes that Forms must be the objects recollected, he cites one of the characteristics which he thinks that Forms possess but sensible particulars do not, when he is trying to demonstrate this nonidentity of the objects recollected with sensible particulars. He claims, in fact, that whenever we see sensible equals, we notice that they fall short of the Form Equal in equality. But there is nothing about the argument for the theory of recollection as such, that leads Plato to cite this specific characteristic to differentiate Forms from particulars, rather than some other respect in which the two differ.

We can see this most clearly if we look at the structure of the argument. We can set this out as follows:[10]

1. Forms have the property P.
2. Sensible things do not have the property P.
3. Therefore sensible things are nonidentical with Forms.

Now in fact, Plato claims that the Form Equal has the property that it is equal, and not unequal, whereas sensible equals have the property that they are both equal and unequal; and from this Plato concludes that sensible equals are not identical with the Form Equal. And Plato indicates that he might make an analogous claim about sensible beautifuls and the Form Beautiful, sensible justs and the Form Just, and so on (75cd). My point is, simply, that Plato might claim, with equal plausibility, that sensible things have the property that they are composite, whereas Forms are incomposite; and conclude from *this* fact, that sensible things are nonidentical with Forms.[11]

Now Plato does not present us with this variation of his argument that I have just suggested. But it does none the less clearly demonstrate the truth of my main contention here – that it would be perfectly possible for Plato to have held a theory of recollection (and of objects recollected) without holding anything recognizable as the theory of Forms. For the theory of recollection does not, in itself, lead us to attribute to the objects recollected any of the properties that are usually said to distinctively characterize Forms. At most, what it requires is that the entities recollected be nonidentical with particulars (i.e. have some property or other that particulars lack), and that they be such as to be known, subsequently forgotten, and finally recollected by the soul. The arguments for the theory of Forms which I discuss in chapters 3 and 4, by contrast, do lead us to attribute a determinate set of properties to Forms (and those normally said to characterize them), as I hope to show in chapter 5. That is why, I believe, we should not say that the argument from recollection that I have assembled on Plato's behalf led him to assume, without argument, the theory of Forms. It may have led him to assume (and it might have led him to argue for) the existence of objects recollected. But we have now seen that this is a very different matter.

We see, then, that though the theory of Forms is closely linked with other new theories in Plato's middle period dialogues, it is none the less logically independent of them. In the same way, I believe, it can be shown that the theory of recollection in the *Meno* – and the theory of Forms in so far as it *is* related to the theory of recollection – is closely linked with the moral interests of the Socratic dialogues, but is none the less logically independent of them.

Forms and Ethics

It is generally agreed among commentators that the *Meno* stands on the borderline between the early and the middle dialogues. So those commentators who stress the continuity of Plato's thought naturally turn to the *Meno* to find evidence of for their view of the origin of the theory of Forms. One of the arguments that the theory of Forms arises from Socrates' concern with ethics runs something like this:[12] the theory of Forms arises from the theory of recollection; the theory of recollection arises from the eristic paradox about knowledge; and the eristic paradox about knowledge arises from an attempt by Socrates to define virtue; so the theory of Forms arises from Socrates' attempts to define virtue (and other moral concepts) and so to rebut relativism in ethics. Now there is only one point I want to make here about this line of thought. And that is, that the eristic paradox about knowledge could arise from an attempt to define any concept whatever, and not just a moral concept. The puzzle is perfectly general. So there is no logical connection between the attempt to define *virtue* and the theory of Forms. Historically, of course, Socrates' or rather Plato's thought did take the course here mapped out. But the point is just that the early steps along the route are far from determining the later ones. The interest Socrates shows in the definitions of ethical terms, does not, either naturally, or inevitably, lead to the theory of Forms.

This has, however, been disputed by Cherniss, who writes, in 'The Philosophical Economy of the Theory of Ideas', that 'the interests of Socrates, the subject matter of the early dialogues, the "practical" tone of Plato's writings throughout all make it highly probable that he took his start from the ethical problems of his day' (p.2). Cherniss sees the early dialogues as showing that 'the definitions requisite to normative ethics are possible only on the assumption that there exist, apart from phenomena, substantive objects of these definitions which alone are the source of the values attaching to phenomenal existence' – all this, 'by demonstrating the hopelessness of all other expedients' (p.3). Now the early dialogues are, of course, largely aporetic in character; and so it is to some extent up to the reader, and the commentator, what moral he chooses to draw from the works. Still, when Cherniss find in the early dialogues what he calls this 'indirect method' (p.5) of proving that there are Forms, he is reading the texts very imaginatively – or at least, his reading would be imaginative, if he were not simply reading into the earlier dialogues the doctrines he finds spelled out in the works of the middle period. This becomes clear, if we compare Cherniss' account of the Socratic dialogues with the much more sober reading of the works offered by Irwin in his *Plato's Moral Theory*.

Irwin is in fact among those commentators who see the theory of Forms as deriving from elements in Socrates' thought. He divides Socrates' moral theory into parts that depend on what he calls elenchos-principle, and parts that depend on what he calls craft-principles (see p.174). The elenchos-principles are largely procedural in character, and it is these that Irwin thinks are preserved in the theory of Forms (in the shape of the theory of recollection, which Irwin thinks is closely related to the Socratic elenchos).[13] But the point that needs emphasizing is the change that Irwin has diagnosed in the use of 'craft-principles' in the middle period. For Irwin has made out a plausible case of believing that Socrates' conception of virtue as a craft performs for him the role that Plato later ascribes to Forms, that of showing how virtue can be justified[14] – and that the theory of Forms in this respect replaces an earlier Socratic theory, and is not, as Cherniss thinks, a mere development of Socratic thought.

The theory of Forms, then, is far from being the natural or inevitable historical sequel to the concerns of the Socratic dialogues. And this is not the only problem with Cherniss' position here. For there is also a very obvious philosophical objection to the line of thought that Cherniss seems to be attributing to Plato. The theory of Forms, on Cherniss' view, is supposed to guarantee a fixed and unchanging moral system; but it is hard to see how it can perform this function if it is to be assumed without argument. It is easy enough to see why Forms must be of a certain character – namely fixed and unchanging – if they are to support ethical values that are fixed and unchanging. But this does not give us any kind of reason to *posit* the existence of Forms. If Cherniss' idea here is that Plato *assumes* the theory of Forms in order to prove (rather than just assume) a fixed and unchanging moral system, it can certainly be dismissed. It is surely unsound scholarship to attribute to Plato such a *petitio principii* on the strength of general conviction about the course of his philosophical development. On the other hand, Cherniss speaks of Plato as being intent on 'saving the phenomena of moral activity' (p.4); and so perhaps – despite the Aristotelian turn of phrase – Cherniss is attributing to Plato the same sort of argument against scepticism about ethics that G. E. Moore employed against scepticism about the external world. If this is indeed Cherniss' line of thought here, it must still be rejected. For in the Socratic dialogues, we find no trace of such an argument.

The most plausible view to hold about the relation of the theory of Forms to Plato's moral theory, then, is that Plato thought that he could prove on independent (non-ethical) grounds that there were Forms (and Forms of moral concepts) of fixed and unchanging character; and that he thought that it followed from this, that there are fixed and unchanging standards in ethics.[15] There is no reason, then, to suppose that Plato would have continued to maintain the theory of

Forms because of his beliefs about ethics, had he ceased to have other grounds for believing in their existence.

Forms and Definitions

I propose next to consider the relation of the theory of Forms to the Socratic interest in definition, and to comment briefly on the views of those commentators who hold that Forms *are* closely linked to definitions, and those who think, by contrast, that Forms are simple nameables, and as such, *not* capable of definition.

Let us first examine the evidence that has persuaded some commentators to adopt the second of these two views, that Forms are elementary nameables, and as such, incapable of definition. This view of the theory of Forms does attempt to explain why Forms have some of the properties that Plato attributes to them in the middle period; but I shall argue that it nonetheless faces overwhelming difficulties, and must ultimately be rejected.

The argument that Plato thinks of Forms as elementary nameables derives from a passage in the *Theaetetus* known as 'Socrates' dream'. In that passage, Socrates discusses a theory of explanation that ultimately depends on the existence of elementary nameables. The argument that Forms are elementary nameables can be set out as follows:[16] elementary nameables in the *Theaetetus* share a number of characteristics with the Forms of the middle period – in particular, both are *monoeides* and *ameriston*. Now these characteristics lead the elementary nameables of the *Theaetetus* to have no *logos*. Forms too have these characteristics; so Forms too have no *logos*. This view of the theory of Forms, then, does derive directly from a study of the properties that Plato ascribes to Forms.

There are, however, overwhelming difficulties with this view. One obvious problem with the view concerns the nature of the relation of the later Platonic text to the theory of Forms. It is not *prima facie* clear that when Plato says in the *Theaetetus* that entities that are *monoeides* and *ameriston* have no *logos*, he is merely repeating what he would have said in the *Republic* had he discussed the question there. It is equally possible that he is criticizing views that he had previously held. The passage in the *Theaetetus* is aporetic, and has been interpreted very differently by different commentators.[17]

Another very serious problem with the view that Forms are elementary nameables is that it is not clear what considerations might have motivated Plato to adopt such a theory. Hicken speaks of it as being a virtue of the earlier theory of Forms that it provides us with ultimate elements of analysis which are comparable with 'true parts of wholes' (p.194); but this is scarcely very persuasive – Plato never says anything like this when he is talking about Forms; and then again there seems to be no reason why ultimate elements of analysis *should* resemble parts of wholes; and finally, it is unclear what Hicken means by '*true* parts of wholes'. It seems, then, that we cannot say that Plato posited Forms as elementary nameables because he thought that elements of analysis should resemble true parts of wholes.

A different view as to why Forms might be thought to be simple nameables has been advanced by Cross (who does not, however, take this view about Forms himself).[18] Cross has suggested that Forms might be supposed to be elementary nameables if they were supposed to be universals. This idea too seems misguided, however. It is by no means obvious that universals are to be seen as elementary nameables; indeed, it is often thought that universals, unlike elementary nameables, do admit of definition (commentators such as Aristotle and Vlastos, for instance, think that Socrates was seeking the definitions of universals).[19] And, in any case, if the idea is that Plato has a theory of Forms where another philosopher would have a theory of universals, then it is surely misleading to discuss this as a theory of elementary nameables.

Perhaps the most serious difficulty for the view that Forms are elementary nameables, however, is the evidence produced in favour of the view that Forms *do* admit of definition. So I shall now discuss this evidence, and the views of those commentators who think that Forms are closely linked with definitions.

Now no commentator, so far as I am aware, has suggested that a Form is nothing more than a definition, or that, if we ask the question, why Plato had a theory of Forms, we should answer, that Plato really had a theory of definitions, and that 'Form' was just his way of saying 'definition'. But I would like, first of all, to examine the position of R. E. Allen on this matter, as some of the claims he makes, in his book *Plato's Euthyphro And The Earlier Theory Of Forms*, might lead the unwary to conclude that Allen at least, does think that there is nothing more to Forms than there is to definitions.

As the title of his book suggests, Allen believes that we find a theory of Forms in the early, as well as in the middle period dialogues; and so he appears to hold an unusually strong view about the fixity of Plato's thought. On closer examination, however, this proves not to be the case. For Allen does not hold that the *same* theory of Forms is maintained in the early and the middle dialogues.[20] In his view, a Form in the early period is just a definition (or, as he likes to put it, an analysis of the essence of something), a universal and a standard to which we may make appeal to settle disputes (see pp. 69-78); in the middle period, Forms retain all these characteristics, but they also become bound up in a new, two-world, ontology, and they start to function as paradigms. In the early period, Allen says, the theory of Forms is essentially continuous with common sense; but in the middle period, it becomes paradoxical (p.109).

Allen turns out, then to hold an unusual view about the theory of Forms. But this is not the view that Forms are nothing more than Socratic universals subject to definition; rather, Allen seems to be proposing that we should extend our normal use of the term 'Form' to cover the objects of Socratic definition, as well as the Forms of the middle period. And this, of course, would be a purely terminological reform. For it is merely a matter of linguistic convention what we choose to call a Form. Some commentators choose to call the 'greatest kinds' of the *Sophist*

'Forms'; others do not. But our choice of terminology here is irrelevant to the substantive question, which is whether or not a 'great kind' in the *Sophist* is, or is not, the same as a Form of the middle period. So too with the relation of the middle period to the early period. R. E. Allen chooses to call the object of a Socratic definition a Form; while other commentators do not. But the important question here is whether a Socratic definition is the definition of the same thing as a middle period Form. And on this substantive question, Allen turns out to agree with all other commentators that it is not.

So let us now ask how the Forms of the middle period *do* relate to the definitions of the early period. I turn first to the widely held view that each individual Form has its own individual definition, and that this is the central feature of the theory of Forms. On this view, it is the definition of the Form, and not the Form itself, that primarily interests Plato, and it is the definition that ultimately performs some of the roles that Plato ascribes to Forms. Now one of the Platonic texts cited in favour of this view is *Phaedo* 96-102; and in so far as this view is related to the theory of explanation that Plato advances in that passage, I shall not consider it here, but in chapter 4 below. But in so far as the view rests on passages where Plato simply expounds, but does not argue for, the theory of Forms, it will be helpful to discuss it here.

The first and most important point I would like to make about this view is that it is obviously incomplete: commentators who take this line must give some explanation of why there is more to Forms than there is to definitions. For if what Plato thinks important is not the existence of Forms themselves, but the existence of definitions of Forms, then it is not clear what a theory of Forms adds to a theory of definitions. If Socrates had already assumed the existence of definitions, and Plato too was really interested in definitions, why, then, did Plato posit the existence of Forms?

In fact, the view that individual Forms have individual definitions, and that this is one of Plato's central claims about Forms, is by no means as well supported from the text as is sometimes supposed. The best evidence for the contention that Forms each have their own individual definitions, is perhaps Plato's use of the phrase *logon didonai* in the middle period. In the early period, Plato uses this phrase, which I will translate as 'to give an account', to refer to giving a definition. He continues to say, in the middle period, that we 'give an account' of Forms. Some commentators then conclude that this refers to giving definitions of Forms.[21]

But of course this conclusion does not necessarily follow from the fact that Plato speaks of giving an account of Forms. For it is perfectly possible that this phrase 'to give an account' could take on different meanings in different contexts. To decide whether ot not this in fact happens, we must examine those passages in which Plato says that it is possible to give an account of Forms. The passages most commonly cited in this connection – *Phaedo* 78d1-2, *Republic* 510d7, and *Republic* 534b3 – have given rise to much exegetical debate. I do not, in fact, have anything new to say about any of them; but it is still worth while to discuss these passages here, in view of the importance attached to them. I shall argue that when Plato speaks of 'giving an account' of Forms, he is not always concerned with giving a definition of individual Forms, but is at least as often concerned with justifying the hypothesis that there are Forms.

Let us turn first to *Phaedo* 78d1-2. Here Socrates refers to αὐτὴ ἡ οὐσία ἧς λόγον δίδομεν τοῦ εἶναι καὶ ἐρωτῶντες καὶ ἀποκρινόμενοι. Vlastos, following Burnet, and followed by Gallop,[22] regards *einai* here as incomplete. Gallop translates 'the Being itself, whose being we give an account of in asking and answering questions'. This is certainly a possible rendering of the Greek; and on this interpretation, Socrates would have in mind the producing of definitions in dialectical debate. But this is not the only possible understanding of the Greek here. It is also possible to take *einai* here to be complete, as Hackforth and Loriaux do,[23] and translate, with Hackforth, 'that very reality, of whose existence we give an account ...'. We may compare *Phaedo* 101de, another passage in which Socrates discusses question and answer in dialectical debate. In *this* passage, it is clear that hypothesis, and not definition, is thought to be the subject of such debate – and the hypothesis in question in this context is in fact the hypothesis that there are Forms. Hypotheses in general, are what the participant in dialectical debate may be asked to give an account of (101d6). We may conclude, then, that Plato's use of the phrase 'to give an account' has changed in accordance with his general view of philosophy. Socrates in the early dialogues is interested in definition; but in the *Meno*, hypothesis, and not definition, becomes the focus of Plato's attention. The ability 'to give an account' remains the mark of knowledge; but Plato's view of what it is to give an account has changed. In the early dialogues, to give an account was to define. But it is indubitable that in *Phaedo* 101de, he no longer means by giving an account, giving a definition, but hypothesizing a hypothesis. And since it is possible to read 78d1-2 so that it accords with 101de, it is clearly preferable to do so.

This development in Plato's thought is confirmed by his remarks on *dianoia* in *Republic* VI. He complains there about the mathematicians that they hypothesize the odd and the even, and so on, but do not think it right to give an account of these hypotheses, either to themselves or to others (thus *Republic* 510c3-d2). Of course, the theory of Forms is what is needed to set mathematics straight here. But while, for the dialectician, the theory of Forms is unhypothesized, for everyone else, it will have the status of a further hypothesis, just as it does in the *Phaedo*; and of this hypothesis, one may be asked to give an account in turn. The mathematicians' terms, themselves hypothesized, would then be explained by another hypothesis, the hypothesis that there are Forms. We find here, then, an application of the method of dialectic recommended in the *Phaedo*, and confirmation that we should think of hypotheses, and not definitions, when Plato speaks of 'giving an account' in the middle period.

When we turn to *Republic* 534, however, we at last find some evidence that Plato has not altogether forgotten about definitions in the middle period. There is a problem with the hypothetical method of dialectic recommended in the *Phaedo*, that a regress of hypotheses will result from the continued application of the method. In the *Phaedo*, Plato simply says about this that we continue to employ the hypothetical method until we reach something satisfactory (101e1). In *Republic* VI, by contrast, Plato introduces us to the Form Good, which is to prevent such a regress of hypotheses from arising.[24] The *Republic* makes it clear that the Form Good stands in relation to the other Forms, as the other Forms stand to particulars: it is their *aitia*.[25] It is the *aitia* of knowledge and truth (508e3-4) not only in the sense that it enables the knower to know the known, but also because it provides to other Forms both *to einai* and *he ousia* (509b6-7): it thus secures the hypothesis that there are Forms, and it is not, itself, hypothesized.

We learn from *Republic* 534b, however, that it does have a *logos tes ousias*. And Vlastos is right, I believe, to think that this form of words here refers to a definition. There are two reasons for this: (a) the Form Good is unhypothesized, and so Plato cannot be referring to a hypothesis here; (b) Plato's use of the word *dihorisasthai* in 534b9 strongly suggests that he has definition in mind. Now in view of the fact that the Form Good is unhypothesized, it is perhaps not especially surprising that it can be defined. But Plato says here that the dialectician can give a *logos tes ousias* not only of the Form Good, but of each thing (*hekastou*, 534b3). It seems, then, that Plato does think that individual Forms can ultimately each be defined.

But it is important not to overestimate the importance of this conclusion. While *logon didonai* certainly does refer to the giving of a definition in this passage, it no less certainly does *not* refer to this, but to the hypothesizing of a hypothesis in *Phaedo* 101de. So it would be a mistake to assume, as R. M. Hare, for instance assumes in his 'Plato and the Mathematicians' (pp. 21-2), that whenever Plato uses the phrase *logon didonai* in his middle period, he intends us to think of definitions. Indeed, we have seen that he more frequently has hypothesis in mind. And although Plato does certainly think that individual Forms do each admit of definition, we have not as yet found any reason to suppose that Plato thought this a particularly significant characteristic of the theory of Forms (I shall return to this question in chapter 4 below). Above all, however, we must remember that Socrates already had a theory of definitions (or believed in the existence and importance of definitions); whereas Plato developed a theory of Forms. And what we want to explain is, *inter alia*, Plato's departure from the ontology of the Socratic dialogues.

Summary

I have now examined a number of attempts to derive a view of the theory of Forms, not from those passages in which Plato argues for the theory, but from passages in which he simply expounds it (sometimes just in passing). I have argued that none of these passages explains why Plato posited Forms as we know them. If Plato had an independent belief in the theory of recollection, that would explain why he posited something – entities recollected – but not why he posited the existence of *Forms*. If Plato was interested in a fixed and unchanging moral system, we can see why he might have been interested in the existence of entities that enjoy some of the properties that he ascribes to Forms (but not all, or the most interesting, of those properties); but it is hard to see how simply assuming the theory of Forms without argument could be supposed to help Plato. If Plato was interested in the Socratic question, and in definition, it is once again hard to see why he should have wanted a theory of *Forms*.

These views of the theory of Forms that are derived from passages in which Plato expounds, rather than argues for, the theory of Forms either fail to show us *why* Plato had a theory of Forms, or why Plato had a theory of *Forms* (rather than entities recollected, definitions, or moral crafts). And perhaps the reason for their common inadequacy as answers to the question 'why did Plato have a theory of Forms?' derives from a common source – namely, the common assumption that Plato never argues for the theory of Forms. For it seems obvious that if we study the arguments that Plato presents for the theory of Forms, we will discover both his reasons for positing the existence of a sort of entity absent from Socratic ontology, and also his reasons for positing the existence of Forms in particular. But if, on the other hand, we do not study these arguments (or if we deny that Plato presents us with such arguments), then it is scarcely surprising that we cannot answer the question why Plato had a theory of Forms.

Of course, not all commentators do take the view that Plato does not present us with arguments for the theory of Forms; and there are those, such as Vlastos and Owen, who *have* made a serious attempt to explain both *why* Plato had a theory of Forms, and why Plato had a theory of *Forms*. I shall discuss the views of such commentators in detail in subsequent chapters; but I should like to say here how I think my approach to the theory of Forms differs from theirs in more general terms. This concerns the emphasis, or lack of emphasis, I place here on assessing the relation of Plato to the philosophical tradition; and it involves distinguishing a third question we must pose if we are to understand why Plato had a theory of Forms – namely, 'why did Plato have a theory of Forms, when other philosophers have not had a theory of Forms?'.

Plato and the Philosophical Tradition

When we examine the accounts of the theory of Forms offered us by Owen and Vlastos, we find, first, that Vlastos (who, as I have already remarked, lays great stress on the definitions of Forms) sees the theory of Forms primarily as an anticipation by Plato of the distinction drawn by later philosophers between the *a priori* and the *a posteriori* (a distinction Vlastos seems inclined to identify with the distinction between the necessary and the contingent).[26] Owen, by contrast, who regards Forms primarily as paradigms, holds that Plato posited Forms because, like Parmenides before him and the early Wittgenstein after him, he had fallen victim to a deep philosophical error about the relation of language to the world, that 'all words behave in the same way'.[27]

Neither Owen nor Vlastos absolves Plato from philosophical error in his theory of Forms. Owen, in fact, believes that Plato's assumption that 'all words behave in the same way' is a mistake, and he also attributes to Plato, as well as this mistaken assumption, an inability to tell identity apart from predication.[28] Vlastos too attributes errors to Plato – he speaks at one point of the theory of Forms as revealing flaws in semantic, logical, ontological and methodological analysis.[29] None the less, Vlastos does think that the theory (*qua* anticipation of the distinction between *a priori* and *a posteriori*) and Plato's arguments for the theory, basically sound. And, if Owen does not think the theory sound, he does at least believe that it is grounded in an important and interesting, albeit mistaken, philosophical assumption, and one that other major philosophers have also found attractive.

It is, in fact, instructive to compare with the views of these two modern commentators, Aristotle's contemporary reaction to the theory of Forms. Aristotle did not have the advantage of a subsequent philosophical tradition in the light of which to assess the theory. But Aristotle too is not content simply to take the arguments for the theory and examine them individually. He too mentions other philosophers he takes to have shared some of the assumptions that contributed to its development. Aristotle's view (which we will examine in more detail in chapters 3 and 4 below) is, in fact, that Plato shares important assumptions with both Heraclitus and Socrates.

So we see that Owen, Vlastos and Aristotle are all concerned to interpret the theory of Forms in terms of deep philosophical ideas that have attracted not just Plato, but other philosophers too – most subsequent Western philosophers if Vlastos is right; Parmenides and Wittgenstein, if Owen is right; or Heraclitus and Socrates, if we believe Aristotle.

Now I do not wish to deny, of course, that Plato does share important assumptions with other philosophers, and in particular, other Greek philosophers. Equally clearly, on the other hand, the theory of Forms cannot be fully accounted for in terms of the assumptions that Plato shares with other philosophers. After all, no other philosopher has posited Forms; but Plato did posit Forms, and this is what commentators are out to explain. The question that interests all commentators, then, 'why did Plato have a theory of Forms?' assumes for me, one last emphasis – 'why did *Plato* have a theory of Forms?', that is to say 'why, given that Plato held certain assumptions in common with any or all of Heraclitus, Socrates, Parmenides, Wittgenstein, and the great majority of western philosophers, does Plato, alone of this set, have a theory of Forms?'.

Vlastos and Owen, do, as we have seen, sketch out their answers to this question. On Vlastos' view, it is presumably Plato's flaws in semantic, logical, ontological and methodological analysis that lead Plato to a theory of Forms and not to a distinction between the *a priori* and *a posteriori*; while on Owen's view, it is presumably the confusion he thinks Plato suffers between identity and predication that leads him to the theory of Forms, rather than to Eleatic Monism or to a picture theory of language. But neither Vlastos nor Owen focus on these aspects of the theory of Forms. I, however, do propose to focus attention in this work on views that I think Plato holds – about real and apparent contradiction – to which few, if any, other philosophers are committed. Unlike Owen, Aristotle and Vlastos, I am primarily interested in asking the question, what gives the theory of Forms its highly individual character.

The suggestion that we can account for much of what Plato says about Forms in terms of his views about real and apparent contradiction has two very general advantages over its rivals, I believe. One of these is, as we will see in chapters 2-4, that it enables us to explain quite a number of puzzling aspects of the theory of Forms at a single stroke. The other advantage is, that it enables us to find some coherency in the theory of Forms. This question is discussed at length in chapter 5. But it is perhaps worth anticipating the argument of that chapter here.

A question traditionally posed by commentators who believe that Plato had more than one reason for positing the theory of Forms, is whether or not the theory of Forms is internally coherent. Cherniss, on the one hand, has suggested that the theory of Forms successfully resolves a number of different philosophical problems, in ethics, metaphysics and epistemology; and he accordingly praises the theory for its 'philosophical economy'. But Cherniss is definitely in the minority here. Cross and Woozley express the typical view of the theory of Forms when they write that 'one of the troubles with the theory, one is inclined to think, is that it is too economical'; and they go on to explain that on their view, Platonic Forms must function both as paradigms and as universals, and that these two roles are incompatible (see pp. 193-4). Thus they find the theory of Forms incoherent. Vlastos, meanwhile, suggests that Plato is trying to draw the *same* general philosophical moral (about logical necessity and physical contingency) from different arguments for the theory of Forms.[30]

Now I shall argue, in due course, that Plato does indeed present several arguments for the theory of Forms, and that there is indeed, as Vlastos suggests, a link between the different arguments Plato presents. But unlike Vlastos, I do not find this link in the general philosophical moral that Plato wishes to draw from the arguments, but in the arguments themselves. For the view I shall advance is that they *all* depend on the *same* view of real and apparent contradiction; and that whatever may be wrong with Plato's view of contradiction, and with the theory of Forms, that it has at least, for this reason, a certain coherency.

Conclusion

I have suggested then, that if we want to understand why Plato had a theory of Forms, we must accomplish three tasks. First we must show why Plato found it necessary to depart from the ontology of the Socratic dialogues; secondly, we must explain why Plato posited the existence of entities that have the set of characteristics ascribed to Forms; and finally, we must ask why Plato took this course when other philosophers have not done so. I have argued further, that the correct approach to the first two tasks is *via* a study of Plato's arguments for the theory of Forms; while we can only hope to accomplish the third task by looking to what is unique among Plato's philosophical beliefs.

NOTES

1. Thus Gallop, *Plato's Phaedo* 95. Commentators often, however, seem to assume without argument either that Plato does or (more frequently) that he does not, argue for the theory of Forms. Moravcsik, 'Recollecting The Theory of Forms', is a rare exception (see esp. 2).

For full bibliographical details of works cited in the Notes or in the text, please see the Bibliography.

2. Crombie, *An Examination of Plato's Doctrines* II 284-9.

3. It is mentioned by Gallop, for instance; and also in Murphy's *Plato's Republic* (111). For a full discussion and criticism of this view, see Nehamas, 'Plato on the Imperfection of the Sensible World'.

4. See Vlastos, 'A Metaphysical Paradox' 52-3, and 'Degrees of Reality' 63-4; R. E. Allen, *Plato's Euthyphro and the Earlier Theory of Forms* 151-4.

5. Gallop 96-7 speaks of Plato as believing that Forms provide a general account of naming and predication when they function as universal, or One Over Many.

6. Gallop 95 points out that in *Phaedo* 75d1-3, and 78d1-2 Plato explicitly connects the theory of Forms with the Socratic question. Cross and Woozley claim that 'the theory of Forms in its ethical aspect is an attempt to account for absolute moral standards' (*Plato's Republic* 185).

7. Moravcsik (3-4) maintains that this passage does contain an argument for the theory of Forms. But he does not analysis the text in detail; and so it is not possible for us to understand wht he has in mind.

8. For a full account of the properties that characterize Forms, see chapter 5 below.

9. Moravcsik (2-3) is surely mistaken when he says that these two questions must be kept apart if the theory is not to be trivial and vacuous. We must postulate entities of a given character, if we are to successfully explain the phenomena that puzzle us. One reason why Moravcsik fails to understand the nature of Plato's arguments for the theory of Forms is that he believes that we cannot derive Forms' properties from the arguments for their existence.

10. This account follows that of Gallop (121-2).

11. It is perhaps worth noting here that although Plato is in fact discussing a case of recollection from likes, when sensible things put us in mind of Forms, this is said not to be significant for the argument (see 74c14-d3).

One complication in the argument is that we must notice the respect in which particulars 'fall short' of

Forms. But it is no less plausible to suppose that we notice that sensible things are composite, than that sensible F's are both F and not-F; and it is no less implausible to claim that we can notice that they fall short of Forms by being composite, than by being both F and not-F.

12. I believe that the following argument represents one strand in Cherniss's thinking in 'The Philosophical Economy of the Theory of Ideas'. Cherniss writes that 'the *Meno* demonstrates how, having to distinguish knowledge and right opinion, in order to save the phenomena of moral activity, the ethical philosopher is forced to face the problems of epistemology' (4).

13. Irwin, esp. 136-140. I do not discuss here this claim, which seems to amount simply to noting that the case of the slave's recollecting in the *Meno* resembles a Socratic elenchos.

14. See Irwin 175.

15. Thus Irwin speaks (154) of assessing the consequences of the metaphysics for the ethical theory. Cross and Woozley (186) also write that Plato's 'is certainly an ethics that has a metaphysical basis' (but see also n.6 above).

16. Thus Stenzel, *Plato's Method of Dialectic* 73. Hicken, 'Knowledge and Forms in Plato's *Theaetetus*' 191-2, tries to substantiate the case for the indivisibility of Forms by adducing further 'indirect evidence'. The view that Forms are elementary nameables was also held by Ryle. See Cross, 'Logos and Forms in Plato' 14; and Ryle's comment in his 'Plato's *Parmenides*' 139: 'substantial Forms were supposed to be just such simple nameables'.

17. Robinson, 'Forms and Error in Plato's *Theaetetus*' argues that Plato now no longer believes that giving an acount is a mark of knowledge. Hicken, Stenzel, and Ryle believe that Plato now no longer thinks it possible to have knowledge of (= to define) Forms, because of their simplicity and indivisibility.

18. Cross 18-9.

19. Cross simply takes this for granted. Compare Vlastos, e.g. 84 n.2; for Aristotle, see *Metaphysics* 1078b.

20. Note in particular the distinction Allen draws (67) between 'a theory of Forms' (which he thinks is found in the early dialogues) and 'the theory of Forms' (which he thinks is not found there).

21. Vlastos, 'Reasons and Causes in the *Phaedo*' 91-2 n.44.

22. Vlastos, *loc. cit.* (n.21); Burnet, *Plato's Phaedo* 66; Gallop 139 (see also 27).

23. Hackforth, *Plato's Phaedo* 81; Loriaux, *Le Phédon De Platon* 164-5. Loriaux aptly compares *Republic* 509b (quoted on p.13 above) for the conjunction of *he ousia* with *to einai*.

24. Whether the 'something satisfactory' of the *Phaedo* anticipates the Form Good of the *Republic* or whether it is just something that is found satisfactory by an opponent in dialectical debate is a traditional, and unsolvable, problem. There is something to be said for both views – which are not, in fact, incompatible.

25. Aristotle confirms this, when he ascribes this role to the One (*Met.* 988a10-11, cf. 987b22-3). The One is identical with the Good, for Aristotle's Plato.

26. 'Reasons and Causes in the *Phaedo*' perhaps gives the clearest statement of Vlastos' view. For a fuller discussion, see chapters 3 and 4 below.

27. For Owen's view, see 'A Proof in The *Peri Ideon*'. Owen draws the comparison between Plato and Parmenides and the early Wittgenstein in lectures and in conversation. The basic idea is that all these philosophers supposed that words all function like names. For Owen's dictum 'all words behave in the same way', compare Wittgenstein, *Philosophical Investigations*, sections 10-12: words 'are absolutely unlike', 'the function of words is as diverse as the function of tools in a tool-box'.

28. 'Notes on Ryle's Plato' 349.

29. 'A Metaphysical Paradox' 56. See also his view that the example of Simmias' height in the *Phaedo* is 'an incidental blemish' on the argument that ('Reasons and Causes' 73) and his view that the 'imitation' or 'copy' theory is a *misconstruction* of universals as a higher level of particular (75).

30. The argument in *Republic* V (in 'Degrees of Reality') and the argument in *Phaedo* 96ff. (in 'Reasons and Causes'). Cherniss does indeed *say* that different arguments establish an interconnection between apparently diverse phenomena (12); but he does nothing to substantiate this claim.

2. CONTEXT AND CONTRADICTION

Introduction

In this chapter, I propose to give an analysis of what is perhaps the most basic and elementary text Plato has given us about the theory of Forms – the discussion of fingers in *Republic* VII, which is designed to lead the novice in philosophy towards being (523a1-3) *via* such Socratic questions as 'what is the big?' (524c10-11).

This passage does not present us with a formal argument for the theory of Forms; but we will find that the considerations Plato advances in *Republic* VII can be turned towards this end – as they duly are at *Parmenides* 129.

My main contention is that the problems presented by these two texts, and others like them, are best explained on the hypothesis that Plato is most directly concerned to confront and resolve a problem of apparent contradiction in these passages; and that he is not primarily concerned to distinguish the logically necessary from the physically contingent, as Vlastos maintains (though I shall argue in chapter 5 below that Plato is in fact committed to the view that certain predicates hold true of Forms essentially); and that the texts do not suggest, as Owen claims, that Plato assumed that all words work in the same way.

'finger', 'big' and 'small'

In *Republic* 523ff., Plato draws a contrast between the different ways in which different sorts of predicate (exemplified by 'finger' on the one hand, and by 'big' and 'small' on the other) apply to sensible particulars; this leads, as we shall see, to the senses' making adequate judgements about one sort of predicate, and inadequate judgements about the other.

We find, when we turn to the text, that Plato is concerned, first of all, to distinguish the contrast he is about to draw from at least one other contrast that he draws elsewhere. As soon as Socrates announces his general thought that there are some things that are adequately judged by the senses without the aid of the intellect, but others that are not, he is interrupted by Glaucon, who thinks he can anticipate what is coming. He thinks Socrates is making a point that is familiar from the *Protagoras*, that we are sometimes deceived by the senses. Socrates says that this is not exactly what he has in mind (523b7), and goes on to give another explanation of his remark that some things are adequately judged by the senses alone, but others are not.

I shall not, however, immediately follow Socrates into this explanation. For it is worth emphasizing the point that when Plato draws a contrast between different sorts of predicate, he is not necessarily drawing the same contrast. There are, in fact, some contrasts between predicates drawn by Plato elsewhere, to which this contrast is not linked, but to which it has sometimes been assimilated.

Thus Irwin, for instance, in the short account he offers of Plato's arguments for the theory of Forms in his *Plato's Moral Theory*, runs together the contrast I am about to discuss, with an earlier, and very different, Socratic contrast between predicates that do not arouse disputes, and those that do (pp. 146-8). In some cases, a definition might serve as an agreed decision procedure to settle a dispute. For Irwin, 'the origin of the trouble is in definitions, not examples' (p.146). The large can be defined; and so disputes about the large can be resolved. Such a resolution, Irwin claims, can not be achieved by the senses alone. 'The senses mingle largeness and smallness, and the soul must distinguish them; to distinguish them, it seeks definitions' (p.147). But then again, Irwin thinks not only of definition, but also of measurement as a potential decision-procedure in this case, and writes that measurement is inadequate, because 'we must know the relevant standard of comparison' (p.148), in order to interpret correctly the size of anything.

It is hard to criticize Irwin's position here, partly because it is hard to know where to start. What needs emphasizing, though, is that we should not lump together different predicate contrasts, in the way that I think Irwin does here. And so I shall simply point to those elements of Irwin's account that figure in other contrasts between predicates Plato draws elsewhere, but which are completely irrelevant to the contrast in *Republic* 523-4. We should note, first, then, that there is no question here, as there is in the *Euthyphro* or the *Phaedrus*, of disputes or agreed decision procedures. Irwin seems to run together the senses' *mingling*, as he puts it, of the big and the small, with *disagreement* about what is big. There is no question of interpersonal disagreement in this passage, or in any of the related passages that I shall be considering. Nor is it easy to see the senses' mingling of big with small as a form of internal disagreement that they might be able to settle by measurement, or with the aid of a definition. A definition may help the intellect; but it seems unlikely to help the senses themselves. And not only will the definition not help the senses themselves, it seems that their problem does not arise from a definition, as we would expect if Irwin's account were correct, but from an example, and not a particularly unusual example that might stretch a definition, either.

So let us return, now, to *Republic* VII, and see what point Socrates *is* trying to make there. Immediately after Glaucon's interruption, he puts his point – a contrast, it will be remembered, between things that *do* and things that do *not* summon the intellect to enquiry – in general terms as follows: Τὰ μὲν οὐ παρακαλοῦντα, ἦν δ' ἐγώ, ὅσα μὴ ἐκβαίνει εἰς ἐναντίαν αἴσθησιν ἅμα· τὰ δ' ἐκβαίνοντα ὡς παρακαλοῦντα τίθημι, ἐπειδὰν ἡ αἴσθησις μηδὲν μᾶλλον τοῦτο ἢ τὸ ἐναντίον δηλοῖ (523b9-c4). I shall paraphrase, in equally general terms, and without, I hope, begging any questions: there are some things such that when we perceive them, we have the perception 'F', but other things such that when we perceive them, our perception can only be represented, and reported to the intellect as 'F/ opposite of F'.

Socrates goes on to give an example, taking 'finger' as his example of the first sort of predicate, and 'big' and 'small' as his examples of the second sort of predicate. He gives at least a partial explanation that I shall not examine very closely for the time being (see *Context and Contradiction*, pp. 30-35 below), beyond noting that the position a finger occupies on a hand does not affect the judgement that it is a finger, in the way that it affects the judgement that it is big or small, or big/small. What I would like to emphasize here is simply the conclusion, first about 'finger': οὐδαμοῦ γὰρ ἡ ὄψις αὐτῇ (the soul, that is) ἅμα ἐσήμηνεν τὸν δάκτυλον τοὐναντίον ἤ δάκτυλον εἶναι (523d5-6). Then about 'big' and 'small', the senses report in just the same way (523e5) as they do about 'smooth' and 'rough'; and about this it says that 'the same thing is smooth and rough' (524a4-5). Again, when Plato moves on to his next example, about one and many, and urges Glaucon to work it out for himself by analogy with this example of the fingers (524d9), he summarizes the moral Glaucon should draw from the dichotomy as follows: εἰ μὲν γὰρ ἱκανῶς αὐτὸ καθ᾽ αὑτὸ ὁρᾶται ... ὥσπερ ἐπὶ τοῦ δακτύλου ἐλέγομεν, εἰ δ᾽ ἀεί τι αὐτῷ ἅμα ὁρᾶται ἐναντίωμα, ὥστε μηδὲν μᾶλλον ἓν ἢ καὶ τοὐναντίον φαίνεσθαι (524d9-e4).

Now this is by way of being an introductory text in philosophy. But there is no mistaking the fact that it presents, for Plato, an important puzzle. For he twice introduces puzzles of exactly the same structure in other dialogues; and he makes the same points about them there too. In the *Phaedo*, Socrates sees Simmias as simultaneously both big and small – big in relation to Socrates, and small in relation to Phaedo; and in the *Theaetetus*, Theaetetus fears that he will say *enantia* about 6 dice that are more numerous than 4 dice, but less numerous than 12, unless he agrees that they have become more (or less), other than by growing (154d2). In both these examples, an observer is inclined to judge 'F/opposite of F' about an object that lies in between two others. Other passages where Plato may also have examples of this sort in mind are *Phaedo* 74, where he says that sensible things that are equal may also be judged unequal; *Symposium* 211, where it is strongly implied that sensible things are both beautiful and not beautiful; and *Republic* 479, where it is agreed that all sensible things that are beautiful, just, holy, double, heavy, and big, will also seem, and be called, the opposite. In the *Phaedo*, Plato does try to say why he thinks that sensible things that are equal may also be judged unequal; but unfortunately, what he says there is ambiguous. We may note, though, that one possible reading of the passage renders the example of the equal sticks and stones there exactly analogous in structure to our example of the fingers in *Republic* VII. In *Republic* V, Plato does not try to say why the sensible things that are just, heavy, and so on, will seem, and be called, the opposite; here, too, though, he may well have examples like the fingers in mind (see further, chapter 3 below). In the *Symposium*, finally, Plato gives a long list of different reasons why sensible beautifuls may also be not beautiful – difference of time, difference of place, difference of relation, difference of observer. Here, the mention of difference of relation clearly links what Plato is saying in *Symposium* 211 with what he is saying in *Republic* VII.

Now the first point we need to notice here is the prominence of the word *enantion* in these passages. The word *enantion* poses problems to the Platonic commentator. C. C. W. Taylor remarks of it that it seems to cover both polar opposite and contradictory, 'together with a number of undifferentiated cases'.[1] But these problems with the word *enantion* need not concern us here. For Plato's use of *enantion* is certainly such that nothing can be both F and *enantion* to F (see my discussion of the law of contradiction in Plato, below pp.35-41). So when the senses make their judgement 'F/opposite of F', the question that most naturally presents itself is whether it is because this judgement is contradictory that the intellect must be called in to help, or whether it is inadequate for some other reason.

Most commentators in fact believe that contradiction is not relevant to the point that Plato is making here. The example of the fingers does not in fact present us with an example of any self-contradictory entity (there are no such entities). And it looks as though Plato must have known this. After all, what he himself says about contradiction, real and apparent, in *Republic* IV, suggests that he knew that difference of relation – like difference of time and difference of respect – is something that enables one and the same thing to carry two apparently incompatible predicates without contradiction. Thus Owen writes of this passage that the predicate 'finger' 'breeds no contradictions that have to be resolved by specifying *pros ti*'.[2] I shall discuss the view taken of our passage by Owen, and also the view of Vlastos, who, like Owen, thinks that contradiction is not Plato's concern here, shortly.

First, however, I would like to discuss the view taken by Cross and Woozley, who believe that Plato himself mistakenly thought that particular sensible things were contradictory, and thus generated for himself unreal puzzles and paradoxes.[3] For this seems to me to be the most intuitively natural view to take of our example (though I believe that it is in fact somewhat mistaken); and it is not so far removed from what I take to be the truth of the matter as is commonly supposed.

Cross and Woozley believe, firstly, that Plato assimilated the predicates that are called interesting in this passage ('big', 'small', 'thick', 'thin', 'rough' and 'smooth') to relational predicates, and that he was unable to distinguish relational predicates from one-place predicates. It is not, in fact, just Cross and Woozley who believe Plato guilty of this assimilation, but also Owen, among others. Owen has remarked that some of the interesting predicates, such as 'large', are actually concealed comparatives, and he has directed attention to *Hippias Major* 288b-289c, a passage that suggests that Plato construed 'beautiful' as really relational.[4] Cross and Woozley remark themselves that Plato treats 'just' in *Republic* I as relational – they write that 'there would be two factors involved' in calling an act 'just', 'the act itself and the circumstances to which it was a response' (p.158).

Now granted that Plato thought the interesting predicates relational, the general idea is then that Plato could have made a mistake about contradiction if he had made a mistake about the logic of relations. Cross and Woozley believe that Plato has said to himself 'x is double and x is half' and has concluded from this that 'x is contradictory'. They point out that a relational predicate cannot be predicated of a single item: 'To predicate a relation of a single term, to say simply "x is double" would be, we would say, to misunderstand the logic of relational expressions; and once we were clear about this, the puzzle Plato finds would disappear' (p.156). Thus if Plato had just said to himself, not 'x is double and x is half', but 'x is double y and x is half z', then he would not have reached the mistaken conclusion, 'x is self-contradictory'.

There are two problems with Cross and Woozley's view. One is, that Plato could distinguish perfectly well between one-place and two-place predicates, as Erhard Sheibe has shown in his article 'Uber Relativbegriffe in Der Philosophie Platons'. (I shall not go into this topic here, as the point becomes very clear from the passage in the *Charmides* which is discussed below on pp.48-54). The other problem is the one I have already mentioned, that in *Republic* IV, Plato seems to think that there are no self-contradictory entities in the world. And Cross and Woozley make no attempt to show how Plato could have combined the belief expressed by Plato in *Republic* IV with the one they find in *Republic* VII, where, on their view, it is implied that there *are* self-contradictory particulars in the world. Their view, then, must be dismissed; and we can conclude on the basis of *Republic* IV, that Plato thought the contradiction he mentions in our passage just an apparent, and not a real, contradiction.

Now those such as Owen and Vlastos who believe that Plato fully understood the apparent contradiction involved in the example we are discussing, do not, of course, believe that that 'apparent contradiction' is the most revealing label for the phenomenon that interests Plato. Thus Owen has termed it 'compresence of opposites', while Vlastos speaks of 'cognitive reliability' and 'degrees of reality'. I now hope to show, however, that there are problems with both these two views of the phenomenon in question, and that we should adopt the view of Prauss, that Plato did not fully understand the contradiction in question here, even though he rightly understood that it is a case of apparent, rather than real, contradiction. I shall argue that both Vlastos and Owen have some difficulty in accounting for the set of examples Plato uses to illustrate the point he is making in these passages.

Let us first examine Vlastos' view. I mentioned in chapter 1 that Vlastos takes the theory of Forms to be one way of stating the distinction between logical necessity and physical contingency, or between the *a priori* and the *a posteriori*; and also that Vlastos finds this distinction in many passages where Plato mentions the theory of Forms. In consequence of this, I shall have to return to his view in chapters 3 and 4, to assess the evidence furnished for his view by Plato's arguments for the theory of Forms from flux and from his theory of explanation. Here, then, I would simply like to spell out his view of the contrast he thinks Plato draws between two different sorts of predication. Vlastos takes Plato to be interested in cognitive reliability, or 'knowledge in an ultra-strong sense of the word',[5] when he complains that sensible particulars such as the finger are such as to be judged 'F/opposite of F'. He states this very clearly in the course of a discussion of *Phaedo* 101-4, in his 'Degrees of Reality'. He there contrasts the proposition

(S1) Simmias is taller than Socrates

with the proposition

(S2) Three is odd,

and comments: 'Now S2 differs from S1 in that radical way whose vast importance for the theory of knowledge Plato was the first to recognize in the history of Western thought. One way of putting this would be to say that S2 takes us out of the domain of contingent truth ... into that of logical necessity ...'.[6]

Now I shall argue in due course that there is another, more plausible reading of the texts that interest us. An immediate problem, however, is posed for Vlastos by the mathematical examples that we may employ to illustrate the phenomenon that interests Plato. Consider the proposition, '4 is double 2 and half 8'. This proposition certainly expresses 'knowledge in the ultra-strong sense of the word'.Yet it shows that, as Plato mentions in *Republic* 479, the doubles, like the bigs, also seem, and are called, the opposite. One objection, then, to Vlastos' view is that the examples Plato uses to illustrate the contrast that interests him actually contradict the expectations it leads us to form. It is just not the case that Plato criticizes all contingent propositions, and sets up logical necessity as a criterion of the truth of propositions. He is equally happy to take his examples of the phenomenon that interests him for the realm of the *a priori*.

Let us now turn to Owen. Owen speaks of the 'compresence of opposites' because he believes that the importance of our phenomenon is that it demonstrates that there are no paradigm cases of what Owen calls 'incomplete' predicates to be found in the world. We can point to paradigm fingers and paradigm men, because no finger is also notfinger, and no man is also notman. But we cannot point to an 'unexceptionable' paradigm of any 'incomplete' predicate.[8] And Owen believes that this interests Plato because Plato believes that all words behave in the same way. Owen sees Aristotle as replying to Plato on this score as follows: 'If "equal" does not behave as tractably as "man" in this world, that does not entail that there is another world in which it does: the use of "equal" is *irreducibly* different from that of "man"'.[9]

Now I do not propose here to discuss the view of language that Owen thinks lies behind the theory of Forms in the middle period. Rather, I hope to show that Owen has as much difficulty as Vlastos in accounting for the range of examples that Plato employs. Plato employs some examples that, on Vlastos' account of the matter, he should not employ. Owen, I believe, has a parallel problem – namely, that there are some examples that Plato should employ, on his view of things, that Plato does not in fact employ. For all relations, of course, are incomplete predicates; but Plato is not interested in all relations alike. 'Big', 'small', 'equal', 'double' – these are a representative sample of the predicates that interest Plato. But 'knowing' figures, along with some of these, on a list of relatives (οἷα εἶναί του) Plato produces in *Republic* 438, and in the *Charmides*, Plato clearly acknowledges that 'seeing', 'hearing', 'desiring' and 'believing' are all relational. Yet he never suggests that any of *these* 'incomplete' predicates presents a problem of the type posed by 'big', 'small' and so on.

Now this criticism of Owen's view if not as immediately telling, as is the parallel criticism of Vlastos' view. After all, Plato could not possibly take every two-place predicate as an example to illustrate his arguments. Moreover, every philosopher naturally returns to certain stock illustrations of his main theses. So it remains quite possible, at this stage of my argument, that Owen is right about the theory of Forms, and that it is just an accident that Plato selects the illustrative examples that he does select. I shall now attempt to undermine the position, by arguing that there are in fact significant logical differences between the two-place predicates Plato thinks of in connection with Forms, and those he does not; and further, that Plato was aware of these logical differences.

The Logic of Relations

If we want to maintain then, that any consideration other than chance is at work here, we must first find some explanation of how the group of relational predicates that Plato definitely finds interesting differs from the group that he seems not to find interesting. I shall take 'bigger' as an instance of a two-place predicate that does interest Plato, and 'knowing' as an instance of a two-place predicate that seems not to interest Plato. I shall discuss their logical differences within the framework of the logic of relations set out by Hodges in his *Logic*.[10] At a later stage, I shall also introduce a distinction made by Bertrand Russell in this field.

A relation is *reflexive*, if every individual has the relation to itself. It is *irreflexive*, if no individual has the relation to itself. And it is *non-reflexive*, if it is neither reflexive nor irreflexive. 'Bigger' is irreflexive; it is, as we shall see, a moot point whether 'knowing' is reflexive, irreflexive or non-reflexive.

A relation is *symmetric*, if whenever an individual b has the relation to an individual c, then it is also true that c has the relation of b. The relation is *asymmetric*, if whenever c has the relation to b, it is false that b has the relation of c. It is *non-symmetric*, if it is neither symmetric nor asymmetric. 'Bigger' is asymmetric; 'knowing' is non-symmetric.

A relation is *transitive*, if whenever b, c, and d are individuals such that b has the relation to c, and c has the relation to d, b has the relation to d. The relation is *intransitive*, if, whenever b, c, and d are individuals such that b has the relation to c, and c has the relation to d, b does not have the relation to d. It is *non-transitive*, if it is neither transitive nor intransitive. 'Bigger' is transitive, while 'knowing' is non-transitive.

A relation is *connected*, if given any two individuals, at least one of them has the relation to the other. In appropriate fields, 'knowing' is not connected, and nor is 'bigger'.

There are certainly logical differences between 'bigger' on the one hand, and 'knowing' on the other, then. 'Bigger' is irreflexive, asymmetric, and transitive; while 'knowing' is nonreflexive (perhaps), nonsymmetric, and nontransitive. So we must see whether Plato was aware of these logical differences, and whether they account for his treating the two groups of predicates differently. I believe that a study of Plato's treatment of the concept of self-knowledge in the *Charmides* will show us that Plato certainly did have at least some awareness of these logical differences between relations; and that it will at least suggest a reason why Plato might have found relations of one sort more puzzling than relations with different logical properties.

Self-knowledge in the Charmides

One of the definitions of *sophrosyne* proposed in the *Charmides* is 'self-knowledge'. Socrates argues that this cannot be right, because 'self-knowledge' is impossible, as he puts it, and because, even if it were possible, it would not be useful. I propose to discuss Socrates' arguments here at some length; for Socrates' contention that self-knowledge is impossible takes the form of an argument that it is impossible to use *any* relation reflexively. Now this in itself betrays an interesting failure to understand relations; but what is of especial importance for my view here is that in the course of his attempt to prove that all relations are irreflexive, Plato makes a distinction between two different sorts of relation. There is one sort of relation that he thinks it is completely impossible to use reflexively, but another sort of relation which does not present quite the same impossibility (see 168e3-4).

The view that all relations are irreflexive is very alien to us; as is Socrates' procedure in this passage taken as a whole. For we can surely just examine the use of any given relation, and decide on that basis whether or not it is reflexive; and if we find (as in fact we do find) that there are any such relations, we can surely dismiss Socrates' view altogether. Socrates' approach to the question is very different. He attempts, by contrast, to show by argument that we do not, indeed cannot, use any relation reflexively: he attempts to derive the irreflexiveness of relations from other properties they possess. This explains why he divides relations into two groups here; for there are some relations which have properties from which it does indeed follow with certainty that they are irreflexive, but there are other relations where this is not the case.

The first group is exemplified by 'bigger', 'smaller', 'double', 'half', 'lighter', 'heavier', 'younger' and 'older'. These relations, which are typical of those that interest Plato in the passages we have been considering, are all both asymmetric and transitive; and because they are all asymmetric, they are all necessarily irreflexive.

Now this is a more sophisticated description of this group of two-place predicates than Socrates himself could give. But Socrates does show some awareness of both the asymmetry, and the transitivity of these relations, as I shall now proceed to argue.

Socrates simply says of the first group, that if we find something that is bigger than the bigger, and bigger than itself, but *not* bigger than what the other biggers are bigger than, it would not only be bigger than itself, but also smaller than itself (168b10-c2). Here Plato exploits (and shows at least some awareness of) the fact that 'bigger' and the other relations that he groups with it are asymmetric. He makes much the same comment elsewhere about the asymmetric relation of 'stronger than', when he argues that temperance cannot be construed as 'self-control': the man who is stronger than himself is also thereby weaker than himself; and for the same reason, *akrasia* cannot be construed as being 'weaker than oneself' (*Republic* 430c-431a; *Protagoras* 355e-356c).

Now recognition of asymmetric relations is not only important for our immediate concerns. Russell, in his *Introduction to Mathematical Philosophy*, has called them 'the most characteristically relational of relations, and the most important for the philosopher who wishes to study the ultimate logical nature of relations' (pp. 44-5). The point is, that it is much easier to construe reflexive relations, such as 'equal', or aliorelatives, like 'unequal', as one-place predicates shared by the individuals that enjoy the relation, than it is to construe asymmetric relations in this fashion. Our present passage in the *Charmides* strongly suggests that at this time at any rate, Plato did make this mistake with reflexive relations and aliorelatives; if he did not, it is hard to explain why he never tries to show that these relations, like the two groups of relations he does consider, are also irreflexive.

Be that as it may, we should just note the evidence here that Plato was aware of the transitivity, as well as the asymmetry of the relations in his first group. It is clearly paradoxical not only that what is bigger than itself is also smaller than itself, but also that the self-bigger, as Plato sets it up, is *not* bigger than what other biggers are bigger than, but *is* bigger than other biggers themselves. Here, Plato exploits (and shows at least some awareness of) the fact that the existence of a self-bigger would render 'bigger' a non-transitive relation, whereas it is, in fact, transitive.

So far, then, so good: Socrates has proved what he might have assumed: but at least his behaviour has been comprehensible. But Socrates obviously cannot derive the irreflexiveness of the second group of relations in the same way; for the second group of relations, exemplified by 'hearing', 'seeing', 'moving' and 'burning', are clearly not asymmetric. And so Plato cannot derive their irreflexiveness from their asymmetry. And they are nontransitive: and so Plato cannot derive paradoxes of the same kind here either. In fact, his behaviour at this point becomes very strange indeed. Before we can hope to understand it, I believe that we must fill in a background assumption that is in play here, and also introduce a further piece of logical terminology.

First, I believe that we can only make sense of Socrates' arguments here if we notice that throughout this section of the *Charmides*, Socrates attempts to model knowledge of one's self (and other selves) after knowledge of *mathemata*. (In the early and middle period, Plato quite often thinks of the relations between people and *mathemata* as standard cases of knowing. See, in particular, *Republic* 438). Clearly, there is normally no problem in individuating *mathemata*; and Socrates' line of approach to the question 'Is self-knowledge possible?', is to ask Critias (who claims that it is) to individuate the *mathema* in question. Critias, quite rightly, wants to reject this demand (166bc), and asserts that it is precisely in having a different sort of object that this sort of knowing differs from other cases of knowing. But, as we shall see later, he is unable to expand on this insight. So much, then, for the general context of the discussion.

The further piece of logical terminology I want to introduce is not used by Hodges, but can be found in Russell's discussion of relations. Russell defines the *domain* of a relation as 'the class of those terms that have the relation to something or other', and the *converse domain* as 'the class of those terms to which something or other has the relation'.[11] Thus we could say, in Russell's terminology, that Socrates is led on to explore the difficulties inherent in what is normally a member of the domain of the relation 'knowing' (i.e. one's self or other selves), becoming, in the case of self-knowing, a member of the converse domain and so displacing the typical member of the converse domain, the *mathema*.

Let us now return to the narrative. Socrates first gains Critias' agreement that there is nothing like self-knowing in the case of other relations – that there is no form of self-seeing of self-hearing, for instance, before he produces any thoughts on why this is so (167c4-168a5). He then, in 168a10-c10, discusses the first group of relations (the asymmetric, transitive relations – see pp.27-28 above) before moving on to the second group, in 168de.

Now no obvious contradiction arises from the reflexive use of the second group of predicates. To be a self-seer, for example, one must also be a self-seen – which seems uncontradictory. The difficulty is supposed to be, that whatever is seen is coloured (168d9-e2), or that in whatever is heard, must itself have a sound (168d4-8). And Socrates apparently thinks it likely that in order to see, one must be without colour, and in order to see, without sound. If that is indeed so, then 'seeing' and 'hearing' are indeed irreflexive relations. There will be a condition that what is seeing must satisfy a one-place predicate incompatible with a one-place predicate that must be satisfied by what is seen. If the case of knowing and self-knowing is parallel to the case of seeing and self-seeing, then there will be a condition on being a knower – I conjecture that this is, for Plato, being a person – incompatible with a condition of being an object of knowledge – I conjecture that we should supply here, being a *mathema*.

But either because Socrates is not certain about these cases, or because he is not certain about generalizing from these cases, he still leaves open the question 'are there any reflexive relations?' (168e-169a). Thus when he discusses the further question 'Is self-knowledge useful?', he allows that a doctor can be both knowing (*qua* doctor) and known (*qua* object of a self-knower's knowledge). But he still makes the point there that a self-knower *qua* self-knower will just know that the doctor is a knower; to know whether the doctor knows medicine, the self-knower would need to know medicine, as well as himself and other selves.

Let us now review the situation. It might seem that this excursion into the *Charmides* has not borne very much fruit. Certainly it shows that Plato did recognize that different two-place predicates have different properties – specifically, that some are, and some are not, asymmetric, and some are, and some are not, transitive. And that suggests in turn that the interest he shows elsewhere in transitive, asymmetric, two-place predicates is not entirely random. But as against this, it might be said that in the *Charmides* Plato seems comparatively clear about these asymmetric transitive relations, and comparatively confused about nonsymmetric, nontransitive relations. So the *Charmides* does not seem to show us why Plato should have found the transitive asymmetric relations especially interesting elsewhere.

But I believe that there is a rather more helpful conclusion that we can draw. For we have seen that Socrates is reluctant to believe – in the case of those relations that are nontransitive and nonsymmetric – that domain and converse domain can overlap, and that this is the source of his conviction that these relations are irreflexive. Now Socrates is right to believe that if the domain and the converse domain of a relation do not overlap, then that relation is irreflexive. But the converse of this is by no means the case. There are many relations that are irreflexive, but of which the domain overlaps with the converse domain. And in particular, this is the case with the transitive asymmetric relations that interest Plato. So if, as I have suggested, Socrates (or Plato) does have some certainty that the domain and the converse domain of a relation should not overlap, then we might expect problems to arise not – where in the *Charmides* he seems most confused – with those relations where, for contingent reasons, such overlap does not arise (seeing etc), but with those two-place predicates where in a field comprising more than two members such an overlap is logically necessary (bigger etc). And the reaction to such problems we would expect from Plato would be some sort of attempt to evade this logical necessity.

Now this is as yet a purely speculative conjecture as to why Plato might have been specially interested in transitive asymmetric relations. In due course, I hope to support it by a study of the controversial texts to which it relates. But before turning to those texts, I would like to answer a question that arises naturally from this speculative explanation, but one that also faces any interpretation of the texts in question. We must try to give some account of what the one- and the two-place predicates that interest Plato have in common.

Context and Contradiction

Now we have already seen how Cross and Woozley, and Owen, answer this question (on p.23 above). And we have now seen why their views are inadequate: they both suggest that more predicates interest Plato than is in fact the case. It is perhaps not surprizing, then, that, as Owen himself has recognized, the label 'incomplete' does not bring out a salient logical feature of the predicates that interest Plato (Owen calls them a 'logical mixed bag' in his 'Notes on Ryle's Plato' p.347). Nehamas has pointed out that they are all either relational or attributive.[12] But this does not take us very far. For Plato surely thought that there was some one characteristic they have in common – and it is this that we want to discover. Evans is one of the most recent commentators to tackle this problem.[13] The form of words he comes up with in answer to the question, that the difference between Plato's two sets of predicates is one of context-dependency as against freedom from context, is, I shall argue, the nearest to the truth.

But let us start from Plato's Greek – and from Owen, who offers his complete/incomplete disjunction as equivalent to the Greek *kath' hauto/ pros ti*. Now the English word 'complete' is the natural complement for the English word 'incomplete'; and the English word 'incomplete' is a reasonable counter for the Greek *pros ti*. So it might seem that 'complete'/'incomplete' represents *kath' hauto/pros ti* well enough. But Plato does not always contrast the *kath' hauto* with the *pros ti*. Sometimes the 'not *kath' hauto*' is not characterized at all (this is the case in *Republic* 524, for instance); and sometimes Plato calls it the *pros heteron*. In particular, in *Philebus* 51cd, Plato slides from contrasting the *kath'hauto* with the *pros ti* (51c7-8) to setting it against the *pros heteron* (51d7-8). Nothing in the argument turns on this move; but it is not what we would expect from a philosopher intent on contrasting complete with incomplete. In *Sophist* 255cd, as Owen himself has pointed out,[14] it is crucial to the argument that the dichotomy lies between the *kath' hauto* and the *pros heteron*, rather than the *kath' hauto* and the *pros ti*. In order to distinguish Being from Different, we need to contrast the aliorelative 'different' with 'being', which does not necessarily imply diversity, but ἀμφοῖν μετεῖχε τοῖν εἰδοῖν (*Sophist* 255d4).

Owen concludes from this that Plato uses the same term, *kath' hauto*, in more than one dichotomy.[15] It is simpler, though, to conclude that there is just one dichotomy here, and that it lies between the *kath' hauto* and the *pros heteron*, rather than the *kath' hauto* and the *pros ti*. The *kath' hauto* would then cover at least some uses of a relational – and hence incomplete – predicate.

This result should be welcomed. For the Greek *kath' hauto*, 'in itself', is naturally complemented by *pros heteron*, 'in relation to other things'. In order to decide whether or not some item may be called *kath' hauto*, we should expect to ask whether or not it can be isolated from other things. In the world of *Theaetetus* 152-160, everything exists only in relation to other things: there is no *kath' hauto* being (157ab). Nothing is anything 'in itself'. In fact, we have just the same use of 'in itself' in English. We may compare the following dictum which Richard Robinson ascribes to motorists: 'speed is not in itself dangerous'. Here, as Robinson remarks,

' "in itself" serves to discount every possible case'.[16] Or, for a closer parallel to the world described in the *Theaetetus*, we may turn to the sceptical doubt expressed by Bertrand Russell at the start of his *Problems of Philosophy*. This leads him to contrast the colour of his table 'in itself' (p.3), with its colour in relation to him, and to other potential observers, and in its relation to the light that falls on it. If we may legitimately say that the contrast here lies between the colour of, in this case, the table, independently of context, and its colour in various contexts, then Evans' term 'context-dependent' illumines the use in question.

It seems fair to say that two contexts are involved both when we call 4 both double (2) and half (8), and also when we say that repaying debts is both just (in most cases) and unjust (when we are returning knives to madmen). In itself, 4 is neither double or half; and nor is returning debts just rather than unjust; but in relation to different contexts, both opposed predicates become applicable. And we can tell the same story about two-place predicates (such as 'bigger than') as about one-place attributive predicates (such as 'big').

The basic ideas here are familiar; but the interpretation of Plato's contrast between different sorts of predicate in terms of context-dependency nonetheless marks a distinct advance in our understanding of Plato's intentions. For it allows us to acknowledge and understand Plato's recognition that not all relations are exactly alike from a logical point of view, and his lack of interest (at least in the middle period) in reflexive relations (see p.28 above). At the same time, it enables us to account for Plato's rather selective interest in relations in a way that other interpretations do not. For not all two-place predicates will be context-dependent – at least for Plato. As it happens there are some two-place predicates which are not context-dependent, and where there is no overlap of domain with converse domain: what is seeing cannot be seen (at least as far as Plato is concerned). For, in order to occupy the first place of this two-place predicate, an object must satisfy the one-place predicate 'colourless' (quite independently of any context), but in order to satisfy the second place in this predicate, it must satisfy the one-place predicate 'coloured' (quite independently of any context), which is incompatible with the one-place predicate 'colourless'. So in this case, we find neither context-dependency, nor overlap of domain with converse demain. Not all two-place predicates, then, are actually context-dependent; it seems that those relations that do not suffer overlap of domain with converse domain are context-independent.

Now my hypothesis is that Plato is interested in context-dependent predicates in so far as he believes that they give rise to problems of at least *apparent* contradiction. Whereas we see that to say that some x is F in one context, but not F in another context is uncontradictory precisely because of the mention here of different contexts, for Plato, the introduction of different contexts simply explains how we are able to attribute apparently incompatible properties to one and the same entity. For Plato, to resolve such a case of apparent contradiction, it is simply not sufficient to point to the fact that different contexts are involved: that is just the origin of the problem. If such cases are to be classified as cases of mere apparent contradiction, some other technique of resolving apparent contradictions will be necessary. And we will see in due course, I believe, how Plato does set about this task.

I shall call this hypothesis about the nature of Plato's interest in context-dependent predicates, the hypothesis that Plato misunderstood the relation of context to contradiction. And I shall argue next that we find instances of this misunderstanding in the *Theaetetus* and in *Republic* II.

At *Theaetetus* 207e7, Socrates asks Theaetetus about a man who is learning to spell, who knows that he should write 'The' in 'Theaetetus', but who gets the same syllable wrong, by writing 'Te', when he comes to write 'Theodorus'. Now Socrates and Theaetetus agree that this man does not yet know the syllable 'The' and that he does not know it, even in the context of the name 'Theaetetus', where he spells the name correctly, and knows how he ought to spell it. The problem that faces the commentators here, is why this man should not be supposed to know Theaetetus' name. If we must say *either* that he knows, or that he does not know the syllable 'The', then we must presumably say that he does *not* know it. But why does Plato not entertain the possibility that he both does, and does not, know it? – that is to say, that in one context he does know it, and in another context he does not know it? The answer I propose to this question runs as follows. For Plato, the propositions 'X knows the syllable "The"', and 'X does not know the syllable "The"', are each, in themselves, uncontradictory. But because our speller knows 'The' in one context, but not in another, we can form the proposition 'X knows the syllable "The" in one context but not in another'. Now to us it is clear that the introduction of the different contexts here removes any appearance of contradiction from this proposition. For Plato, however, the introduction of the qualification 'in different contexts' simply explains why we have a problem of apparent contradiction here, but does not resolve our difficulty.[18]

Another case where Plato may well betray a misunderstanding of the relation of context to contradiction occurs in *Republic* II. In 375b, Socrates says that it is now clear what properties of mind and body are required in an auxiliary. He remarks to Glaucon, however, that there is a problem here. Auxiliaries, it seems, must be gentle with their fellow citizens, but harsh with the enemy (375c1-4). 'What shall we do? Where will we find a character that is at the same time *praion* and *megalothumon?*', asks Socrates, giving the explanation that the *praieia physis* is opposed to the *thumoeides* (375c7-8).

Now this is clearly a philosophical problem; but it does not receive a philosophical solution here, but rather a practical refutation. Socrates simply returns to a comparison he has previously drawn between auxiliaries and dogs, and remarks that dogs do have these opposites (375d7-8); and so it evidently is possible, and not against nature, to have such a character. Socrates does not, however, tell us *how* this is possible.

What is of interest here, is not simply that Plato does not resolve his philosophical problem in philosophical terms, but also the fact that he should find it at all difficult to believe that there can be those who are hostile to one set of people, but friendly towards others. For there does not seem to be any problem here, to us. I believe that we should once again here explain Plato's problem then as arising from a misunderstanding of the relation of context to contradiction. Plato finds it *prima facie* contradictory to have opposed dispositions towards different sets of people; and so he is inclined to think that it is impossible. But he is prepared to yield, on this point, to the facts of the world.

It is a similar problem, I believe, but one Plato does tackle philosophically, that interests Socrates and Glaucon in *Republic* VII. We saw some time ago (pp.21-22 above) that some things lead the senses to judge 'F/opposite of F', while others do not. I would now like to consider in detail the explanation Plato gives us of this phenomenon. In fact, Plato makes his point here twice – once about 'finger', and once about 'big' and 'small'. Of 'finger', we learn that it makes no difference to the senses whether it is seen in the middle or at the end, whether it is pale or dark, thick or thin, and so on (523c11-d3). The context, then – the position of the finger on the hand etc. – makes no difference to the senses' judgement that it is a finger. In fact, nothing affects this judgement. The contrast with 'big' and 'small' follows in 523e3-5 – τὸ μέγεθος αὐτῶν καὶ τὴν σμικρότητα ἡ ὄψις ἆρα ἱκανῶς ὁρᾷ, καὶ οὐδὲν αὐτῇ διαφέρει ἐν μέσῳ τινὰ αὐτῶν κεῖσθαι ἤ ἐπ' ἐσχάτῳ; asks Socrates. As Kirwan has pointed out, both parts of this question should receive the same answer – and that answer is 'no'.[19] Plato is saying that sight does *not* adequately see the size of the fingers, and that the position of a finger does *not* make no difference to sight's judgement as to its size. The context, then, does not affect the senses' judgement as to whether or not the finger is a finger. But it does affect their judgement as to whether or not a finger is big or small, and it may thereby render such judgements unsatisfactory.

The following picture then emerges. We perceive three fingers, the little one, the second one and the middle one (523c5-6). Perception gives a clear and satisfactory verdict about all the fingers, that they are fingers; and it also gives clear and satisfactory verdicts as to the size of the two fingers that lie *ep' eschatoi*, at the end – it reports, no doubt, that the little finger is small, and that the second finger is big. But about the middle finger, the senses bear an opposed, and unsatisfactory report – namely that it is both big and small. And the reason for this is that the senses observe it in two different contexts, and in the context of the little finger, the middle finger is big, while in the context of the second finger, it is small.

Now we are bound to find this a strange result. For we all know perfectly well that it is not in fact a mistake on the part of our senses to make allowances for context in our judgements about size. In fact, it is only because we do make such allowances, that when we judge the same thing both big and small, such a judgement is not contradictory. For Plato, however, it seems that a judgement is satisfactory if, like 'x is a finger', it makes no reference to context; and some judgements that make reference to context, like 'the little finger is small in relation both to the second, and to the middle finger', are also satisfactory. But other contextual judgements, such as 'the middle finger is small in relation to the second finger, but big in relation to the small finger', which involve the attribution of opposed properties to one and the same thing, are unsatisfactory – and unsatisfactory for the reason that they are *prima facie* contradictory.

This view of the matter is, I believe, strongly supported by the account Plato goes on to give, in *Republic* VII, of the intellect's response to the unsatisfactory judgements of the senses; and also by the resolution he offers us, in *Phaedo* 102, of the analogous problem he presents there about Simmias' height. Before considering these passages, however, I would first like to examine the evidence that has led many commentators to believe that Plato understands the topic of contradiction exactly as we do ourselves, and consequently to reject this view of the text of *Republic* VII.

Plato and the Law of Contradiction

In *Republic* IV, in the course of his argument that the soul is composed of different parts, Plato writes at one point Δῆλον ὅτι ταὐτὸν τἀναντία ποιεῖν ἤ πάσχειν κατὰ ταὐτόν γε καὶ πρὸς ταὐτὸν οὐκ ἐθελήσει ἅμα, ὥστε ἄν που εὑρίσκωμεν ἐν αὐτοῖς ταῦτα γιγνόμενα, εἰσόμεθα ὅτι οὐ ταὐτὸν ἦν, ἀλλὰ πλείω (436b8-c1).

Numerous commentators have taken this to be Plato's formulation of the law of contradiction, and the forerunner of Aristotle's formulation of the law in *Metaphysics* Γ. Now this law tells us that *p* and not-*p* cannot both be true; and so anyone who acknowledges the law thereby acknowledges that the world is uncontradictory. If Plato is indeed formulating the law of contradiction here, then, it would seem that he cannot, as I have suggested, believe that the problem with the senses' judgement about the middle finger is that it is a contradictory, or *prima facie* contradictory, judgement.

Let us ask first, then, whether Plato is indeed formulating the law of contradiction here. Richard Robinson has suggested that the principle Plato announces here (which Robinson calls 'The Principle Of Opposites') is rather different from our law of contradiction. In the first place, Robinson says, the Principle of Opposites is 'very unlike' the law of contradiction because 'our law of contradiction is a statement about propositions, and propositions only'; whereas Plato does not make it clear what range of entities is covered by his principle – he speaks only of 'the same thing ... doing or suffering', and this suggests that he does not have propositions in mind ('propositions do not appear to do or suffer anything'). And in the second place, Robinson writes, 'Plato's Principle of Opposites differs greatly from our law of contradiction in not being about contradiction, but about opposition. Contradiction belongs to propositions, and is precise. Opposition belongs to a great many things, and is vague'.[20]

Now both Robinson's points here are incontrovertible; but Robinson perhaps overestimates their significance. For the differences he mentions between the Principle of Opposites and the law of contradiction do not seem to matter, either for our understanding of the argument in *Republic* IV or for our present purposes. In the argument in *Republic* IV, as we shall see, Plato invokes the Principle of Opposites where we would invoke the law of contradiction; and in the context of that argument, it seems equally legitimate to invoke either principle. And as for our present concerns, we must admit that the Principle of Opposites is just as incompatible with the account I have offered of the problem that interests Plato in *Republic* VII as is the law of contradiction.[21] For the senses there judge that the middle finger is big in relation to the little finger, but small in relation to the second finger. And in *Republic* IV, Plato seems to know that if we say that something is F in one respect but not F in another, or F in relation to one thing, but not F in relation to another, or F at one time, and not F at another, then what we are saying is not contradictory, or even *prima facie* contradictory.

But there are in fact other possible interpretations of what Plato is saying in *Republic* 436ff., which would render this text perfectly compatible with the interpretation I have offered of *Republic* VII.

We must consider, first of all, the possibility that Plato is not trying to present us here with our law of contradiction, or with a perfectly general Principle of Opposites, but with a very limited princple about contradiction, and one that does not have any bearing on the passage that interests us in *Republic* VII. In fact, Plato says in *Republic* IV, simply that the same thing will not do or suffer (or be, 437a1) opposites in certain circumstances (at the same time, in the same respect, and so on). And he presents this as a hypothesis which might conveivably be mistaken (437a4-10). He says, then, that certain states of affairs do not, in fact, seem to occur. But he does not say *why* such states do not occur. We may contrast the law of contradiction as we have know it since Aristotle. For this law tells us that certain states of affairs are not possible because they are contradictory: that contradictory states of affairs are not possible. And it presents this, not as a hypothesis subject to possible disconfirmation, but as a necessary truth.

Now Plato undoubtedly saw the same link between possibility and contradiction as we do ourselves: what is possible is not contradictory. But perhaps Plato is not trying here in *Republic* IV to deal with all cases of apparent impossibility or apparent contradiction. Plato says in *Republic* 436 only that it is not possible for the same thing to be both F and not-F in certain circumstances (as the same time, in the same respect, and so on). He does *not* say whether or not he thinks it is possible for the same thing to be both F and not-F in other circumstances (at different times, in different respects, and so on).

Commentators take it for granted that Plato does not mention these other states of affairs, because they are so manifestly uncontradictory. My suggestion is, however, that he does not mention these states of affairs, because he thinks they are contentious, and that their analysis is complicated. They clearly are possible – as everyone, in the face of the facts, would agree. And if they are possible, they must be uncontradictory. But perhaps it is not easy to see why they are uncontradictory. Perhaps such states of affairs are apt to confuse the senses, and only an intellect on the road to the theory of Forms could give a clear account of such matters.

So it may be, then, that the principle Plato announces in *Republic* 436 covers only *some* of those states of affairs that he is inclined to think contradictory – those that he is most certain really are contradictory, and consequently impossible. If it is indeed the case (as I believe the evidence suggests) that other states of affairs also seem *prima facie* contradictory to him – if he thinks that it is *prima facie* contradictory that the second finger is smaller than the middle finger, but bigger than the little finger, but that this is nonetheless a possible state of affairs, and one that a philosopher might understand, such cases are just not his concern in *Republic* 436.

But even if it were granted that Plato is, with his Principle of Opposites, attempting to formulate our law of contradiction, it still would not follow that what he says here in *Republic* IV conflicts with what I represent him as saying in *Republic* VII. For, as Prauss has argued convincingly in his *Platon und der logische Eleatismus*, Plato in *Republic* IV in fact shows a rather insecure grasp of the topic of contradiction in general; and in particular, of the means of resolving apparent contradiction.[22]

Prauss says, correctly, that Plato's formulation of the law of contradiction resembles Aristotle's; but that the real question is, whether Plato understands the law of contradiction in the same way as Aristotle (pp.94-5). To answer this question, we must examine Plato's argument in *Republic* IV in detail, and see how much understanding Plato does manifest there of real and apparent contradiction.

Plato gives a number of examples there of apparent contradiction, which are intended to illustrate various facets of the law of contradiction, and at the same time, to confirm its validity. These examples extend from 436c5-437a2; they all concern the incompatible predicates 'moving' and 'at rest', apparently applied to the same thing at the same time (436c5-7).

The first example concerns a man who is at rest, but who is moving his head and his hands. In this example, Prauss notes, we would expect Plato to invoke the *kata tauton* qualification to resolve the apparent contradiction. Plato, however, says of him that one part of him is at rest, another part is moving (436c11-d3). On these grounds, Prauss remarks that he does not know what the *kata tauton* qualification in Plato's formulation of the law of contradiction is; but he does know what it is not – it is not the same as the *kata tauton* qualification in Aristotle's formulation of the law (pp.95-6).

The second example, that of a spinning top both in motion and at rest, is also somewhat puzzling. For once again, Plato does not employ the means to resolve the apparent contradiction we would expect. We would expect Plato to make some mention of relativity in his resolution of this apparent contradiction. In fact, however, the resolution Plato offers us once again seems to involve specifying different parts of the apparently contradictory entity as the true bearers of the incompatible predicates in question. What he actually says is that the top is moving with respect to (*kata*) its circumference, but at rest with respect to its axis (436e1-3). Thus technically he resolves the apparent contradiction by the use of the *kata tauton* qualification. But it is difficult to see this as a separate and independent technique for resolving apparent contradictions. For it seems to come to much the same thing to say of a man that his arms are in motion but his body is at rest, as to say that he is in motion with respect to his arms, but at rest with respect to his body. Similarly, it seems to make no difference whether we say that part of the top is at rest, and part in motion, or whether we say that the top is at rest with respect to one part of itself, but in motion with respect to another part of itself. And this is a rather surprising result – we would expect these two examples to illustrate different ways of resolving apparent contradiction. And what is no less surprising, is that Plato's attempt to resolve this apparent contradiction is, in fact, simply wrong. As Cross and Woozley remark, 'in the sense in which any *part* of a vertically spinning top is in motion, every part is; the fact that the top does not move from the spot on which it is spinning or incline out of its vertical axis does not mean that the *whole* top is not moving on that spot. Relativity of motion does not necessitate that different *parts* of the objects are in motion and at rest respectively' (p.116).

Plato does not give any examples here of how the other two qualifications on the law of contradiction, *hama* and *pros tauton*, may serve to resolve apparent contradictions. Indeed, he seems to set aside the law of contradiction in 437a, and make some points about relations, before turning to the case of the thirsty man, the example that really interests him.

That, at any rate, is the usual account of Plato's procedure here. But it is an account on which I would now like to cast some doubt. For, on the one hand, the *pros tauton* qualification obviously concerns two-place predicates and contradiction; and on the other hand, Plato goes on after 437a to introduce some two-place predicates, and make some further points about contradiction. (That, after all, is why he makes these further points here, after he has introduced his hypothesis about contradiction, but before the example of the thirsty man, which is the goal to which the discussion is directed.) In these circumstances, it may be correct, I believe, to take what Plato says in 437a very literally. What he is doing, is just taking his hypothesis about contradiction as established, and promising to look at it again, if any further examples are produced. He does not intend us to think that he is setting aside the whole topic of contradiction, or that he is not discussing the *pros tauton* qualification, when he introduces the principle of the qualification of relatives in 438a.

This principle says that if one of a pair of relatives is qualified in some way, the correlative expression must also be qualified in some way (though not necessarily in the same way). To take one of Plato's examples, if a is bigger than b, then b is smaller than a; but if a is *much* bigger than b, then b is *much* smaller than a.

We can see how the principle enables us to clear up cases of apparent contradiction, if we consider another example Plato gives us in this passage. Let us suppose that a is *about to be* bigger than b (see 438b11-12). It may be false that b *is* smaller than a. What is true is that b is *about to be* smaller than a.

So, if my conjecture here is right, and the principle of the qualification of relatives is indeed the *pros tauton* qualification in disguise, then Plato thinks that it serves to resolve those apparent contradictions that arise, if we qualify one of a pair of relatives, but neglect to qualify the other. In that case, the *pros tauton* qualification in Plato's hypothesis about contradiction would be very different from the *pros tauton* qualification in Aristotle's citation of the law of contradiction, and Plato would here show no awareness of the function of the *pros tauton* qualification that appears in Aristotle's formulation of the law of contradiction.

Be that as it may, however, we must now consider the two final cases of apparent contradiction that Plato discusses here. These are both to be resolved by positing nonidentical subjects as the real bearers of the incompatible predicates in question. The case of the archer, who draws back his bow with one hand, but draws it forward with the other (439b8-11) needs no glossing. But the case of the thirsty man is more complicated. I shall argue now that Plato's presentation of this case is, once again, very puzzling.

This case, like the case of Leontius which follows it, could be presented as an example of *akrasia*. As such, it arises from a Socratic background. For Socrates, as we have seen (p.28), denied the existence of *akrasia* partly on logical grounds: a man who is stronger than himself is also weaker than himself, and as such is contradictory. Plato will agree with all this. The idea of a man who is stronger than himself is indeed contradictory. So he proposes instead the picture of a man whose reason is stronger than his emotions (or *vice versa*).[23]

He takes the case of a man who wants to drink, and also wants not to drink. He wants to drink because he is thirsty, and thirst just is desire for drink (439a1-3). We are not told why he wants not to drink: Glaucon just agrees with Socrates that sometimes people who are thirsty nevertheless do not drink (439c2-4). Let us fill in some details for ourselves, then, and consider, with Crombie, the case of a man who is forbidden to drink by his doctor, because he has dropsy.[24] He is thirsty, but he knows that drinking will be bad for him. In this situation, he will either be self-controlled (and not drink), or akratic (and drink). If he makes the judgement that, all things considered, he should not drink, he is in the state that seems to interest Plato. He is thirsty; but nevertheless does not drink.

It might seem, then, that Plato has here a simple and effective argument for the view that the soul is composed of separate parts. Thirst leads men on to any form of drink, good or bad (see 439a1-3). But sometimes, a man's intellect says to him that he should not drink, even when he is thirsty. It seems, then, that two agents are at work here: the man is both led on to drink, and restrained from drinking. But leading on and restraining are incompatible (437b). And so the soul is composed of separate parts.

Despite its straightforward appearance, however, this argument presents us with at least one serious puzzle. This concerns the nature of Plato's response to an objection to his argument that he discusses in 438a. Here, he imagines an interlocutor maintaining that all desire is for the good, and so all desire for drink is desire for good drink (our dropsical patient would be a man for whom no drink is a good drink).[25] Now Plato's reply to this move consists in a straightforward application of his principle of qualification of relatives – he says, in fact, that thirst as such is desire for drink as such, and not for some specified sort of drink (439a).

Now what Plato says here deserves careful scrutiny. For it is at about this point that Richard Robinson seems to have found a flaw in Plato's argument. Robinson believes that the argument depends on a confusion between psychology and semantic analysis. He argues that the principle that 'thirst itself for drink itself and not for any special sort of drink' is a truth of logic, if it is a truth at all; but that Plato mistakenly treats is as a truth of psychology. 'It can never tell us', he writes, 'what kinds of liquid people do in fact thirst for, and what kinds they reject' ('Plato's Separation of Reason from Desire', p.42).

And we can reinforce Robinson's sense that there is something wrong with Plato's argument at this point, by noting that while drinking is a relation, thirsting is not necessarily relational. Quine, in his 'Quantifiers and Propositional Attitudes' has drawn a distinction between two possible readings of the proposition 'Ernest is hunting lions'.[26] If Ernest is hunting some particular lions, Quine treats the proposition as relational and 'hunting' as a two-place predicate true of Ernest and the lions he is hunting. But if Ernest is hunting lions as he might be hunting unicorns, then Quine calls the predicate 'notional', and 'hunting lions' becomes a one-place predicate true of Ernest. Now it is not hard to see that 'drinking' is always and necessarily relational, but that 'thirsting', like 'hunting lions' will sometimes figure in relational propositions, and sometimes in notional propositions. It is possible to be thirsty, and yet to reject all the drinks to hand, as not what one is thirsting after.

Let us now try to apply these insights to our example of the dropsical patient. The patient is thirsty, and this means that he wants to drink; but as Robinson maintains, this tells us nothing about what sort of liquid he wants to drink. In the case we envisage, perhaps just the one-place predicate 'wanting a drink' is true of the patient. On the other hand, the patient wants, all things considered, not to drink – and this expresses the relational proposition, that of any drink, our patient wants not to drink it. Plato has thought that the two desires, to drink and not to drink, are contradictory, when in fact we can see that they are not. If the patient had had two desires, to drink and not to drink, directed at one and the same object, then we might be facing a case of real contradiction. But as things stand, those who, whilst thirsty, nevertheless do not drink, are not living counter-examples or even apparent counter-examples to the law of contradiction, or to Plato's hypothesis about contradiction. We must conclude then, that Plato does not fully understand the case of thirsty men who fail to drink. Thirst as such may be for drink as such; and some thirsty men nevertheless don't drink; but this does not give rise to a contradiction requiring division of the soul into component parts.

What, then, is the upshot of this discussion of what Plato says about contradiction in *Republic* IV? Does it show that Plato understands real and apparent contradiction just as we do ourselves? I have argued that the truth is far otherwise. We have seen, first, that Plato's hypothesis about contradiction here is not the same thing as our law of contradiction. At the same time, Plato clearly agrees with us that those states of affairs that are possible, are *ipso facto* uncontradictory; and we learn, from *Republic* 436, that Plato further agrees with us that it is contradictory (and so, not possible) for the same thing to enjoy opposed properties at the same time, in the same respect, and so on. But, I have argued, for all Plato says in *Republic* 436, he may still find other states of affairs, which he would agree to be possible, *prima facie* contradictory; and he may still not understand the true reason why these states of affairs are not, in fact, contradictory.

I have argued, further, that the examples of apparent contradiction Plato discusses in *Republic* 436-9, strongly suggest that Plato's grasp of this topic is generally insecure; that Plato shows an undue propensity to resolve apparent contradictions by positing the existence of parts in entities that enjoy apparently incompatible attributes; and in particular, that he simply does not understand the example of the thirsty man properly. I have also suggested a way of taking the *pros tauton* qualification that would involve us in attributing to Plato a very different understanding of it from Aristotle's.

So I would now like to return to *Republic* VII, and examine the intellect's response to the problem posed for it by the reports of the senses. I shall argue, following Prauss, that the intellect's resolution of the problem, and Socrates' analogous resolution, in the *Phaedo*, of the analogous problem there about Simmias' height, strongly support the contention that Plato does not understand the true reason why such states of affairs are uncontradictory.

The Resolution of the Contradiction and the Theory of Forms

We left *Republic* VII, when we had seen how the problem there is set up – that the senses are criticized there for making inadequate judgements, and that the reason for this is the weight they allow to context. So let us now ask how the intellect sorts out the inadequate reports of the senses. Plato does not set out here the full course of the intellect's reflections on this matter; but he does show us the intellect's first – and, I think, quite telling – reaction to the report of the senses, that the same thing is both big and small.

The first question that the intellect asks is εἴτε ἓν εἴτε δύο ἐστὶν ἕκαστα τῶν εἰσαγγελλομένων (524b5). Now on Owen's view of the passage, or on Vlastos' view, this is a very strange response to the report that 'the same thing is big and small'. We would expect the intellect first, perhaps, to note that this is not a self-contradictory report, and then to seek either an unexceptionable paradigm of big and small (on Owen's view), or (on Vlastos' view) a contrast between physical contingency and logical necessity. On my view, however, it is perfectly natural that intellect asks the question, whether each of the things reported is one or two. The intellect asks this question, simply because it is trying to make sense of the apparently self-contradictory report it has received from the senses. And it is pursuing, naturally enough, Plato's own favourite method of resolving apparent contradictions, that of positing the existence of 'logical' parts in the apparently self-contradictory object. Following up this line of enquiry, the intellect next decides that the two things are separate (κεχωρισμένα, 524b10-c1, διωρισμένα 524c7), whereas the senses judge them to be one thing, mingled together (συγκεχυμένον τι, 524c7). As a result of this, we are told, the intellect is led to ask the question 'what is the big?' (524c11).

Now it is not clear, on any account of the matter, why the intellect is led by such experiences to ask Socratic questions. But we can, at least, see the relevance of such enquiry. For the intellect's investigations will lead it either to the Form Big itself, or at least to a definition of the big. And we can then see that the intellect will make uncontradictory judgements about each of these entities, while the senses will continue to make apparently contradictory judgements about the size of sensible fingers. (I shall discuss the question of the intellect's judgements about the sensible world in chapter 3.)

Republic VII, then, neither supplies us with a full account of the intellect's reasoning about these matters, nor with a full resolution of the apparent contradiction involved in the senses' report on the size of the middle finger. It does take us some of the way towards this latter objective, though; and the hints it provides as to how the apparent contradiction should be resolved are supplemented by the rather fuller account Plato gives us in *Phaedo* 102, of the case of Simmias, who, like the middle finger in the *Republic*, occupies a position intermediate between something bigger than him (Phaedo), and something smaller (Socrates). Like the middle finger, he too is called both big and small (ἐπωνυμίαν ἔχει σμικρός τε καὶ μέγας εἶναι, 102c10-11; cf 102b2: τούτων τὴν ἐπωνυμίαν ἴσχειν). Just prior to the explanation he gives of the example of Simmias here, Plato has introduced the theory of Forms as explanations (I discuss this at length in chapter 4); and he tells us now that we can explain Simmias' height by saying that he partakes in two Forms, Big and Small (102c10-d4). That, no doubt, is the conclusion to which the intellect in *Republic* VII will in due course arrive. For the purpose of our comparison, though, what we should note is that Simmias is said here to have two things *in* him – λέγεις τότ' εἶναι ἐν τῷ Σιμμίᾳ ἀμφότερα, καὶ μέγεθος καὶ σμικρότητα (102b5-6) – referred to in 102d5ff. as the big in him and the small in him. And these, I believe, are the 'logical' parts of Simmias that truly bear the incompatible predicates 'big' and 'small'. Certainly, the big in Simmias and the small in Simmias are not merely unfortunate turns of phrase, but are thought of as real entities. For Plato says of them that like Forms, but unlike particulars, they will never admit the predicate that is opposed to them. And this fact, it seems to me, indicates that the big in Simmias and the small in him, form a part of what Plato thinks there is, just as surely as do the Forms Big and Small, and the particular big and small things.

We may conclude, then, that the middle finger in *Republic* VII and Simmias in the *Phaedo* present a real problem of apparent contradiction for Plato, in so far as Plato has misunderstood the relation of context to contradiction. He has not seen that it is precisely because it is in different contexts that particulars bear incompatible predicates that they are not self-contradictory; rather, he seems to think that it is because particulars can be seen in different contexts that they are apparently self-contradictory. Faced by this unreal problem he resolves the apparent contradiction he finds here by positing that the subject of the incompatible predicates is composed of logical parts that are the real bearers of the predicates.

If this is right, the theory of Forms is not an essential feature of the resolution Plato offers us of the apparent contradiction in question. All that is necessary is that we recognize that things in the sensible world are composed of logical parts. And neither in *Phaedo* 102 nor in *Republic* 523-5 does Plato seem to be advancing a formal argument for the theory of Forms, though he does think the theory of Forms relevant in both cases. As we have seen, the puzzle in *Republic* VII should lead the intellect towards being, and hence presumably towards the theory of Forms; and in the *Phaedo*, we learn not just that there is a big in Simmias and a small in Simmias, but also that he participates in the two Forms Big and Small. And the theory of Forms plays an even more prominent role in another text, *Parmenides* 129, where an exactly analogous difficulty of apparent contradiction does seem to be presented as an argument for the theory of Forms. For there, no mention is made of logical parts; the theory of Forms alone, it seems, suffices to resolve the difficulty. We must ask, then, what relation the theory of Forms does have to this problem of apparent contradiction in the sensible world, and to the logical parts in particular, that have hitherto seemed to us sufficient to resolve this difficulty.

Let us then turn to *Parmenides* 129, and examine this text more closely. The problem Plato is discussing there arises from an argument against plurality attributed to Zeno, which is set out in 127e: if there were many, they would be both like and unlike (no completions are supplied), and that is impossible (127e1-2). οὔτε γὰρ τὰ ἀνόμοια ὅμοια οὔτε τὰ ὅμοια ἀνόμοια οἷον τε εἶναι (127e3-4). It will not now come as a surpise that Plato (and Plato's Zeno) seems to think that nothing can be both like and unlike (completions or no completions). What does seem surprising, is that when Socrates turns to resolve this problem in 129ab, he does not rely on positing the existence of logical parts in particulars, but on positing the existence of Forms. Thus he says in 128e6-129a3: οὐ νομίζεις εἶναι αὐτὸ καθ' αὑτὸ εἶδός τι ὁμοιότητος, καὶ τῷ τοιούτῳ αὖ ἄλλο τι ἐναντίον, ὃ ἔστιν ἀνόμοιον · τούτοιν δὲ δυοῖν ὄντοιν καὶ ἐμὲ καὶ σὲ καὶ τἄλλα ἃ δὴ πολλὰ καλοῦμεν μεταλαμβάνειν. In that case, it is, Socrates tells us, because of participation in the Form Like, that we are all like, and because of participation in the Form Unlike, that we are all unlike (129a3-6). And it is not at all surprising that it is possible for the many to participate in both these two opposed Forms (129b1). Similarly, Socrates says, we would all agree that it is possible for the many to participate in both the two opposed Forms, One and Many (129b3-d6).

Now the question that interests us is whether the resolution of the difficulty Socrates presents here, which depends on the existence of Forms and participation in them by the many, is the same as the resolution of the difficulty we saw in the *Phaedo* and the *Republic*, which depended on the existence of logical parts in particulars. Whether these two resolutions are really the same, or whether they are, as they appear, different, is a hard question. For the answer depends entirely on the nature of participation; and this is deliberately left vague by Plato when he first introduces the notion; it is never subsequently spelled out, and it comes under attack in the *Parmenides*. But we can learn something, I believe, from the form taken by the attack on the notion of participation in the *Parmenides*. The crucial point is that the view of participation attacked in the *Parmenides* is one that depends on an analogy with physical parts.

In the *Phaedo*, Forms are presented as the explanations, in some sense, of sensible particulars. In the *Parmenides*, Plato poses the question how the explanation works. Here, it is argued, a *whole* Form cannot act as explanation in the case of each particular; we cannot each have the whole Form in us (131bc). It would seem, then, that we are each e.g. big, in virtue of a *part* of the Form Big that we each have in us (131c5-8). This too, however, leads to obvious difficulties, if we take the suggestion literally (131c9-e2). Socrates and Parmenides finally conclude, then, that participation is not possible *either* κατὰ μέρη *or* κατὰ ὅλα (131e3-5).

Now it is reasonable to suppose that Plato is producing an objection here to a view that he himself had held, or at least found attractive. And if this is so, then I think we can see what relation the positing of Forms in which we participate might have to be positing of logical parts in us. We might conjecture that the existence of logical parts in us is simply what constitutes our participation in Forms – that for x to participate in the Form Big, for instance, is for there to be in him a logical part that is big, and in no way small.[27] If this is so, it is easy to see how our immediate conclusion from observing the apparent contradiction involved in our fingers, that there are logical parts in them that are truly big and small, could lead us on to the further conclusion that there are Forms in which we participate, and which are represented by these logical parts in us. We can see, then, why Plato may have had a special reason for believing in the existence of Forms of those things that are not as they seem (*Parmenides* 131d3-4).

But at the same time, we must recognize that this is not Plato's only, or most important reason for believing in the existence of Forms. I shall argue in chapters 3 and 4, that Plato has two general arguments for the existence of Forms, identified by Aristotle as the argument from flux, and the argument from explanation; and that these arguments would lead Plato to believe in Forms of everything, and not just of those things that are not as they seem. I hope to show that both these arguments manifest precisely the same view of the relation of context to contradiction as the one examined here – that in the argument from flux, Plato takes particulars to seem contradictory (to all those who have no knowledge of Forms) because they bear different, and incompatible, predicates at different times; and that in the argument from explanation, he takes our ordinary explanations to be contradictory precisely because he does not see that in one context, we expect one explanation, and in another context, a different one.

NOTES

1. *Plato's Protagoras* 128.

2. 'A Proof in the *Peri Ideon*' 307.

3. See Cross and Woozley 154-160.

4. Owen, 'Proof' 306.

5. 'cognitive reliability' – see 'A Metaphysical Paradox' 49; 'knowledge in an ultra-strong sense of the word' – 'Degrees of Reality' 69.

6. 'Degrees of Reality' 68.

7. *Plato*, see esp 156, 175 and 188. Gosling distinguishes (158) between 'day-to-day' knowledge and 'true knowledge' (he italicizes these phrases). In fact, Gosling criticizes Plato very strongly for his concept of knowledge (see 288-9).

8. Owen, 'Proof' 310.

9. Owen, 'Proof' 311.

10. See 174-186.

11. Russell, *Introduction to Mathematical Philosophy* 32.

12. Nehamas, 'Predication and Forms of Opposites in Plato's *Phaedo*' 470. This point is also made by Brentlinger, 'Incomplete Predicates and the Two-World Theory of the *Phaedo*' 70 n.12.

13. Evans, *Aristotle's Concept of Dialectic*, see 101.

14. See 'Plato on Notbeing' 256-8.

15. 'Plato on Notbeing' 257. Julia Annas has pushed the same line of thought further, and has tried to develop three distinct dichotomies here ('Forms and First Principles' 267 n.3). The three different contrasts are (*a*) a *pros ti* item is a relative to which another item is correlative; (*b*) a *pros ti* item is incomplete, making no extractable independent contribution to a sentence; (*c*) a *pros ti* item is one which is essentially *alio*relative. Annas remarks 'these different contrasts are never clearly distinguished by Plato, or by Hermodorus, or anyone else in the Academy'; this alone, I believe, must cast some doubt on the validity of her schema. So too must the fact that, on her view, the roles of the *kath' hauto* items 'fall together' (as she puts it), whereas the different *pros ti* roles fall apart. This suggests that she has simply not understood what Plato's various uses of the term *pros ti* have in common.

16. 'Plato's Separation of Reason from Desire' 48. Robinson points out that Plato uses the idiom 'in itself' very extensively in *Republic* I.

17. We find paradoxes of apparent contradiction involving the predicates 'knowing' and 'notknowing' in *Euthydemus* 293bd, and in *Theaetetus* 163e-164a. In neither of these cases, surprisingly enough, does Plato explicitly tell us how to resolve these contradictions. It may be, however, that Plato intends the reader to solve the puzzles Plato has set him with these paradoxes by making distinctions between various means of knowing, or the various different *mathemata* one can know. Thus in the *Theaetetus*, the point may well be that we can distinguish between 'knows by hearing', 'knows by sight', 'knows by touch', and perhaps 'knows by remembering' (compare Macdowell's commentary, 162-3). In the *Euthydemus*, the point may well be the Socratic insistence on the relational nature of knowledge – Socrates is always complaining that sophists claim to impart a knowledge that, by contrast with *technai*, has no correlative subject matter (thus *Protagoras* 312). Socrates is forever asking questions like 'But what is this knowledge or what is it of?' (*Laches* 194e4). Thus perhaps the puzzle in the *Euthydemus* is to be resolved by making a distinction between knowledge of one *techne* and knowledge of another – one can be an archer but not a carpenter.

18. The peculiarity of this passage was first noted by M. F. Burnyeat, 'Aristotle on Understanding Knowledge' 135-6. Burnyeat sets down the peculiarity to a tendency on Plato's part to assimilate knowledge to understanding – what is a mistake about knowledge is not necessarily a mistake about understanding. This reading of the passage is clearly possible; and whether we prefer this interpretation or that offered in the text above will depend largely on how plausible we find the general views of which the interpretations form a part.

19. 'Plato on Relativity' 122-3. One instance of the opposite view can be found in Crombie **ii** 294-5.

20. These quotations are all drawn from p.39 of 'Plato's Separation of Reason from Desire'. Irwin (*Plato's Moral Theory* 327 n.18) follows Robinson on both counts.

21. Robinson says it 'pretty clearly conflicts with a passage in the next book' (39).

22. See 93-9.

23. It remains a moot point whether or not contradiction is involved in the analysis of *akrasia* or not. Davidson, in 'How is Weakness of the Will Possible?', suggests that the concept be analyzed in terms of two *prima facie* reasons for action, which do not contradict one another, and a third, unconditional,

judgement as to what is best, all things considered, which in its turn does not conflict with either of the two *prima facie* reasons for action (see esp. 106 and 110). Davidson does not try to show what *does* motivate akratic action; he is content to say that it is not motivated by reason at all (112).

24. Crombie I 345.

25. Irwin, *Plato's Moral Theory* 327, construes the objection as 'one desires drink as a good', rather than, 'one desires good drink'. But this makes Socrates' response to the objection, with the Principle of Qualification of Relatives, rather off-beam. 'I desire a big drink' cannot be treated in parallel fashion as 'I desire drink as a big'.

26. See 101-2.

27. Thus also Nehamas 'Predication and Forms of Opposites in the *Phaedo*' 477. The idea of 'logical parts' as a key to the *early* dialogues is mentioned by M. Furth, in 'Elements of Eleatic Ontology' 259. If Furth is right about this, the middle period dialogues follow the early dialogues by taking this idea more literally.

3. THE ARGUMENT FROM FLUX

Aristotle's Evidence

Aristotle says that Plato's theory of Forms arose on the one hand, from his belief in a flux theory, and on the other, from Socrates' interest in definition. In this chapter, I shall examine the first of these two claims. I shall argue that Aristotle is right in identifying one of Plato's arguments for the theory of Forms as an argument from flux; and that the argument in question exhibits a misunderstanding of contradiction (as well as the acceptance of a flux theory).

In *Metaphysics A*, at 987a32-b1, Aristotle tells us that Plato, both when he was young, and also later, believed the Heraclitean opinion that all sensible things are in flux (ἀεὶ ῥεόντων), and that there is no knowledge concerning them. In *Metaphysics M*, at 1078b12-18, he gives us a fuller account of his view of the matter, and he reports an argument for the theory of Forms that runs as follows: all perceptible things are in flux (ἀεὶ ῥεόντων), ὥστ' εἴπερ ἐπιστήμη τινὸς ἔσται καὶ φρόνησις, ἑτέρας δεῖν τινὰς φύσεις εἶναι παρὰ τὰς αἰσθητὰς μενούσας · οὐ γὰρ εἶναι τῶν ῥεόντων ἐπιστήμην. Ross sets out the argument Aristotle reports here as follows: if knowledge exists, there must be unchangeable objects of knowledge. Knowledge does exist. Therefore there exists an unchangeable object. Sensible objects are changeable. Therefore there exist non-sensible realities.

Now Ross suggests that this argument is in fact to be found in the text of Plato – in *Timaeus* 51-2, and *Republic* 479-80;[2] and I shall argue in due course, as against the views of some more recent commentators, that Ross is right about this. To this end, I should now like to point to three distinctive features of this argument as Aristotle reports it that will, I believe, help us to reidentify it in these Platonic texts.

The first point concerns the conclusion of the argument, 'there exist non-sensible realities'. Annas remarks about the argument, in her commentary, that 'the nearest Plato comes to accepting something like the argument from flux is at *Timaeus* 51-2, where he does accept that the physical world is in flux, and that therefore objects of knowledge cannot be found in it. But the *Timaeus* assumes, and does not argue, that the latter are Forms'.[3] Now Annas may have hit on a real difficulty in the argument here (though I believe that the difficulty is not in fact as great as it may seem): the argument purports to prove that there are Forms, but all it does show is that there are 'non-sensible realities' in Ross' terms, or objects of knowledge not in the physical world, and not in flux. But this difficulty, such as it is, is common to both the Platonic and Aristotelian versions of the argument, and so does not distinguish the two.

The second distinctive feature of the argument concerns the direction of the proof. An epistemological premiss, 'there is knowledge' gives rise to an ontological conclusion, 'there are Forms': if we were to deny that there is knowledge, the argument would no longer provide us with any reason to believe that there are Forms.[4] This may seem surprising, in so far as the direction of the *inference* here is not the same as the direction of the *causation* that is sometimes thought to be involved. Bolton, for instance, writes about the *Phaedo*, that there 'the mutability of physical objects is responsible for their epistemic status'.[5] And some such thesis plays an important part in the argument here too. None the less, the main thrust of the argument is that, if there is knowledge, there must be objects of knowledge. And I shall argue in due course both that Plato too, commonly draws ontological conclusions from epistemological premisses, and also that he draws *this* ontological conclusion, that there are Forms, from the epistemological premiss that there is knowledge.

The third distinctive feature of the argument here is the strange claim, which has attracted much attention from commentators, that there is no knowledge of the physical world, because it is in flux. This seems to argue a strange view, either of knowledge or of the physical world, on Plato's part – if Aristotle's account of the argument is right. I shall argue about this claim, finally, both that Aristotle is right to find it in Plato, and that it is not to be explained by a strange view of the physical world, or a strange view of knowledge, but rather by a strange view of contradiction – a view for which we have already assembled some of the evidence in chapter 2.

Now some commentators simply do not find the argument reported by Aristotle anywhere in the Platonic corpus. Owen, for instance, has suggested that an argument for the theory of Forms from flux is a natural extension of the argument that he attributes to Plato for the theory of Forms, an argument from the compresence of opposites.[6] Owen believes that Plato concentrated on the qualification *pros tauton* in this argument for the theory of Forms, as we have seen in chapter 2; but Owen notes that Plato does also recognize the parallel between this form of qualification and the temporal qualification *hama*. (We find the two mentioned side by side both in *Republic* IV and in *Symposium* 211). If we notice that all predications are (implicitly) temporally qualified, then we can say that all earthly applications of predicates will manifest compresence of opposites – what is 'finger' today will be 'notfinger' next century, for instance. So we have the same need of a paradigm here in the case of the predicate 'finger' as we find with the more obviously 'incomplete' (because relative or attributive) predicates.

Now Owen does here produce an argument for the theory of Forms from flux; but it is certainly not the same argument from flux that Aristotle attributes to Plato in *Metaphysics M*. Owen neither exploits nor explains the strange claim that there is no knowledge of the sensible world. In fact, his argument makes no mention whatever of epistemological considerations. So we see that Owen is really saying that Aristotle has missed Plato's main line of thought, and that his version of the argument from flux is not historically accurate.

Other commentators find Aristotle's evidence easier to accommodate. For Vlastos and Gosling, an argument from flux for the theory of Forms consistutes an important part of a more general argument about the nature of knowledge. For Gosling, as we have seen, Plato just had an unusually strong set of conditions for knowledge, one of which was the absence of temporal qualifications from all propositions expressing knowledge; for Vlastos, these conditions indicate that Plato was intent on distinguishing the *a priori* from the *a posteriori*, and restricting knowledge to the *a priori*.[7] Both these commentators thus do try to come to terms with the claim that we do not have knowledge of the sensible world – by ruling that for Plato, temporally qualified propositions do not express real knowledge, or that *a posteriori* knowledge is not real knowledge. But this position is still very unsatisfactory in so far as it still leaves us the problem of explaining why Plato had this strange conception of knowledge.

Two recent commentators, Bolton and Irwin, who have taken Aristotle's evidence very seriously, have focused their attention on Plato's view of the physical world, and the concept of flux involved in the argument. Now it is clear that the argument does depend, *inter alia*, on some specifix conception of the physical world. So I propose to examine these commentators' (very different) views rather more closely, and ask what Plato did think about the stability of the sensible world. For if we can get clear about this, we will be better placed to answer questions about the argument from flux. In particular, we will be able to see whether (as Bolton maintains) Plato believes that there is no knowledge of the physical world simply because he has an unusual conception of the physical world.

Plato and Flux

We can divide ancient philosophers into those who allow just rest (Eleatics), those who allow just motion (Heracliteans), and those who allow both rest and motion. This threefold division is made by Plato himself in the *Sophist* in a passage where he argues that a philosopher should follow the third option, and admit both motion and rest in his ontology (246-250). But some commentators believe that this had not always been his opinion. Bolton in particular, in his article 'Plato's Distinction between Being and Becoming', has recently argued that Plato had held a Heraclitean theory until he refuted such theories in the *Theaetetus*, and that the argument for the theory of Forms in *Republic* V depends on such a Heraclitean theory.

He produces some textual evidence to support this view from the *Phaedo* as well as from *Republic* V itself. In the *Phaedo*, Plato says that particulars are 'just about never constant with ... respect to themselves in any way' (78e3-4), while in the *Republic*, he says that 'they are no more *whatever* anyone may affirm them to be than not' (479b9-10).

But does Plato mean what he says in these passages? In particular, are they strong enough to support Bolton's contention that Plato admitted no rest whatever into particulars in the middle period? For the view that absolutely nothing is at rest is a very surprising view indeed, as a number of commentators have pointed out. Gosling writes that it 'requires one to take "change" very strongly, so that the wall is in flux only if the moment after our dubbing it a wall, it has ceased to be white, a wall, the same shape, coloured ... the supposed world would be a bewildering place'.[8] Bolton puts essentially the same point in terms of 'patterns of becoming'.[9] On his view, these passages justify us in attributing to Plato the view that not only are particulars always becoming (e.g. white) rather than being (e.g. white), but also their very 'patterns of becoming' (e.g. their becoming white) are themselves in flux.

I shall approach the question whether he is right, by posing two other questions, both prompted by Irwin's article 'Plato's Heracliteanism' – 'what is a flux theory?' and 'why should a philosopher adopt a flux theory?'.[10] Irwin, like Bolton, thinks we should take Aristotle's evidence very seriously, and like Bolton, he identifies the argument in *Republic* V as the argument from flux. Unlike Bolton, though, he takes the view that no physical change whatever is involved here. He has, needless to say, an odd view of what consistutes a flux theory.

In fact, he believes that either what he calls 'self-change', or what he calls 'aspect-change' counts as evidence of a flux theory, at least as far as Heraclitus, Plato and Aristotle are concerned. ('Self-change' covers all real physical change. 'Aspect-change', 'a reduced and metaphorical kind of change',[11] covers 'Cambridge' change, and change of relation.) This enables him to count the doctrine of the unity of opposites in Heraclitus as the evidence of his flux theory, and the Platonic doctrine of the compresence of opposites as the evidence on which Aristotle ascribed to him both a flux theory, and Heraclitean influence. He further claims that even if Plato nowhere explicitly distinguishes s-change from a-change, this does not necessarily mean that he was confused between them. In the middle period, Irwin believes, Plato was just interested in a-change, and s-change plays no part in the argument for the theory of Forms from flux.[12]

Now Irwin's central contention rests on a simple error. Even if the evidence he has assembled did show that this trio of philosophers 'do sometimes refer to a-change when they speak of flux' ('Plato's Heracliteanism', p.6), this still would not imply, as Irwin thinks, that 'talk of flux does not require reference to s-change' ('Plato's Heracliteanism', p.12).

A flux theorist might well not deny the existence of a-change. But it is hard to see belief in a-change as a distinctive characteristic of flux theory. For a-change is not incompatible with rest; and a flux theorist must surely argue against the existence of rest. For if a flux theorist believes that 'there is s-change, a-change, and rest', it is hard to see how he differs from the next man. Yet the ancient philosophers certainly were familiar with the doctrine that there is no such thing as rest. Plato has Socrates introduce such a flux theory in the *Theaetetus*. And if we examine this dialogue, we will see that this doctrine does present a strange and distinctive view of the physical world; that such a doctrine must be supported with argument; and what sorts of arguments are adduced in its favour.

First, though, let us see how a flux doctrine differs from our normal beliefs. Irwin has drawn an interesting comparison between the view of personal identity advanced by Socrates there, and the very different view expressed by Diotima in the *Symposium*.[13] Diotima believes that Socrates is 'called the same from a youth until he is an old man' (207d5-6), despite his undergoing the usual physical changes of mind and body in the meantime. Socrates in the *Theaetetus*, by contrast, suggests that he should be regarded as a series of stages, such as Socrates-ill, and Socrates-well (159b3-4), which are dissimilar, and hence non-identical (159b10). Now why is there this difference of opinion between Diotima in the *Symposium* and Socrates in the *Theaetetus*?

If we mean by this question, simply 'why does Plato express these two inconsistent views?', then the answer may be that only in the *Symposium* is Plato speaking *in propria persona*; and the conflict between the two views shows us that we should be wary of attributing to Plato himself any of the views expressed in *Theaetetus* 152-160.[14] But the question can also be interpreted more philosophically, as meaning 'why is it that the flux theorist takes a different view of these phenomena from Diotima?'. And the answer to *this* question, I believe, must be that the flux theorist, unlike Diotima, has a general reason of unrestricted scope that is independent of all observation, for believing that everything is in flux. And it is this that comes into play here, and leads him to regard the change in Socrates as entailing a loss of personal identity. Diotima can give particular explanations of all the changes she admits in the world – in the case of Socrates, for example, his changing can be accounted for by his eating of food as he passes from youth to manhood. The flux theorist, on the other hand, will not need a particular reason to be given before he concludes that a particular like Socrates is undergoing change in any respect. He has, instead, a general reason for thinking that Socrates is undergoing change of identity all the time.

So if we ask, now, what motivates the flux theory in the *Theaetetus*, we are asking what general reason of unrestricted scope Socrates produces there for thinking that everything is always changing. The answer is very clear: Theaetetus' ontological position is determined by his epistemological position. It is only an extreme, or (to borrow Crombie's term) 'rampant' flux theory that will support the epistemological thesis 'knowledge is perception'. If we accept the epistemological premiss 'knowledge is perception', we must accept the ontological conclusion 'the world is in rampant flux'. (For only if the world is in rampant flux will perceptual judgements fail to be intrinisically liable to correction.) But of course we need not accept the epistemological premiss; and in that case, we will have no reason to believe that the world is in rampant flux.

But Socrates does also take steps to render the flux theory plausible, independently of the epistemological thesis that knowledge is perception. And it is also instructive to examine these manoeuvres, if we want to see what sort of consideration might prompt a philosopher to adopt a doctrine of rampant flux.

We have already seen the not entirely implausible Heraclitean view of personal identity Socrates advances there, which leads on to an excellent account of dreams and madness. That aside, Socrates employs a good deal of rhetoric, notably in his praise of change (152d-153d). Above all, though, we have the example of Socrates and the dice.

The changes that Socrates and the dice undergo are not self-changes, but aspect-changes, in Irwin's terminology. Unlike Socrates' changes in health and personal appearance, they are not real changes at all, and so strictly speaking, do not belong here at all. They are, however, introduced as examples of self-change. The basic thinking involved is simple: Socrates has changed aspect, and 'small' rather than 'tall' has become true of him. Now Socrates has undoubtedly changed. Yet we cannot explain this change in physical terms – Socrates has not, say, shrunken in the meantime. We must conclude then, that there are inexplicable (physical) changes going on in him, that we would not readily suspect. This line of thought not only converts the apparent aspect-change into a self-change; it also supports an extreme, or rampant, flux doctrine. For once we admit the existence of such inexplicable and unexpected changes in Socrates and the dice, the question inevitably arises, how widespread such changes are. Conceivably, only a few individuals or only a few predicates might be involved. But simplicity, in the absence of other considerations, will tell strongly in favour of our accepting a flux theory of unrestricted scope.

We find, then, two distinct sorts of motivation given for the flux theory in the *Theaetetus* – on the one hand, an epistemological thesis, and on the other, a metaphysical puzzle. Both support an unrestricted, rampant, flux theory (i.e. one that allows just motion, and no rest at all), in so far as both provide us with a general reason for thinking that everything is in flux.

And it is not just when he is setting the theory up in the *Theaetetus* that Plato shows his awareness that he is dealing with an extreme flux theory, but also in his refutation of the theory there and in the *Cratylus* (this point has often been noted, most recently by Bolton). The argument in the *Cratylus* at 439-440 represents a less sophisticated version of the argument in the *Theaetetus*, as Cherniss notes in his 'The Relation of the *Timaeus* to Plato's Later Dialogues'.[15] There are two features common to both versions of the argument, both of which show that Plato is combatting a rampant flux thesis. The first of these may be termed a second wave of application of flux theory. In the *Cratylus*, Socrates remarks that if everything is in flux, then so too is 'knowing' as well as sensible particulars (440ab). In the *Theaetetus*, precisely the same point is made, but initially about 'seeing' and 'hearing' (182e1-4), which leads to 'knowing' by a simple substitution on the 'knowledge is perception' thesis. This second wave of application of flux theory is only legitimate, if the flux theory in question is of unrestricted scope. The other feature common to *Cratylus* 439 and *Theaetetus* 181-3 is a comparison of the speed of flux with the speed of speech – *Crat.* 439d8-11; cf. *Tht.* 183a9-183b5. And this too, is only legitimate if the flux theory attacked is a rampant flux theory. For only such a theory could support the application of the view that there is flux to the 'patterns of becoming', which in the *Theaetetus* (though not in the *Cratylus*), Plato sees is a necessary preliminary to this comparison.

This study of flux has not as yet enabled us to draw any direct conclusions about Plato's own view of the physical world. It has demonstrated, though, that argument is required to establish an extreme, or rampant, flux theory; and we have seen what sort of argument Plato thinks appropriate to this end in the *Theaetetus*. But Plato nowhere presents us with any argument in favour of such a flux theory on his own account. Rather, he seems to regard the view he takes of the sensible world (whatever it is) as the intuitively obvious one. We should not, then, I believe, attribute to him the highly paradoxical view that there is just motion in the world, and no form of rest whatsoever, simply on the basis of the rather casual remarks Bolton cites from the *Phaedo* and the *Republic*.

But Bolton, of course, does not just urge these theses texts as the evidence in favour of his view. He also claims that the argument in *Republic* V is unintelligible, unless we suppose that Plato did hold a rampant flux doctrine (pp.77-80). Let us see now whether this claim is justified.[16]

I shall in fact argue that Plato's argument in *Republic* V manifests the same misunderstanding of the relation of context to contradiction that we have already witnessed in *Republic* VII and elsewhere. I shall approach the argument in question, however, by way of the argument for the theory of Forms in *Timaeus* 51-2, which resembles Aristotle's reconstruction of the argument from flux more closely than the argument in the *Republic*. I hope to show that in neither case must we assume any stronger thesis than the thesis that all things in the world are constantly becoming rather than being (and from this point on, I shall use the term 'flux' to refer to this normal constant change in the world, and not to describe the doctrine that there is no form of rest whatsoever in the world). In both cases, we will find that the ontological thesis, that there are Forms, is deduced by Plato from the epistemological thesis, that there is knowledge, and that the claim that there is no knowledge of the sensible world plays a crucial role in the argument. Finally, in neither case will we find Plato making any attempt to show that the entities whose existence he purports to prove here are the same as the Forms whose existence he purports to prove elsewhere.

The Argument in the Timaeus

The argument for the theory of Forms in the *Timaeus* is just as compressed as Aristotle's report of it in the *Metaphysics*. It runs as follows: εἰ μὲν νοῦς καὶ δόξα ἀληθής ἐστον δύο γένη, παντάπασιν εἶναι καθ' αὑτὰ ταῦτα, ἀναίσθητα ὑφ' ἡμῶν εἴδη, νοούμενα μόνον · εἰ δ', ὥς τισιν φαίνεται, δόξα ἀληθὴς νοῦ διαφέρει τὸ μηδέν, πάνθ' ὁποσ' αὖ διὰ τοῦ σώματος αἰσθανόμεθα θετέον βεβαιότατα (*Timaeus* 51d3-7).

Once again, we find here that the argument moves from an epistemological premiss, 'mind and true belief are to be distinguished', to an ontological conclusion, 'there are *kath'hauta* entities'. Once again, we find that if we deny the premiss, we no longer have any reason to believe the conclusion. In fact, this time we are told that if mind and true belief are not distinct, an ontological consequence does follow, but a different ontological consequence: in that case, we must posit a very stable physical world. When we recollect that in *Theaetetus* 152-160 we are asked to posit a physical world in rampant flux, in order that our perceptual judgements of it should constitute knowledge, we may be inclined to think that there is no restraint on what ontological conclusions Plato thinks we can draw from epistemological premisses.

The argument once more presupposes that there is not, in fact, any knowledge of the sensible world, because it is not stable. It is not immediately clear, either from the passage quoted above, however, or from the wider context, quite what degree of instability Plato is here attributing to particulars. The doctrine that there is an epistemological distinction between knowledge and true belief on the one hand, and an ontological distinction between the sensible world and the world of Forms, on the other, is first introduced, in 27d-28a, as follows: τὸ μὲν δὴ νοήσει μετὰ λόγου περιληπτόν, ἀεὶ κατὰ ταὐτὰ ὄν, τὸ δ' αὖ δόξῃ μετ' αἰσθήσεως ἀλόγου δοξαστόν, γιγνόμενον καὶ ἀπολλύμενον, ὄντως δὲ οὐδέποτε ὄν. Plato's initial introduction of his view here certainly does make it clear that there is a complete disjunction between two classes of entity, 'what *is*' and 'what *becomes*'. But, as our previous discussion has shown (cf. p.51), this in itself does not take us very far. As Bolton has noted, 'this language does not commit Plato to the extreme view of becoming which is defeated by the argument in the *Theaetetus*' (p.90). It does not commit him to a flux of 'patterns of becoming', nor, *ipso facto*, to a fundamental disagreement with the majority of mankind about the description of the world.

But some remarks Plato makes later in the dialogue might seem to promise us a more rampant flux doctrine than is suggested by the introduction of the view. In *Timaeus* 49, Plato might seem to say that what is just *becoming* never admits the description *touto* or *tode*, but can just be called *toiouton*. In 50ab, he goes on to draw an analogy between the sensible world and molten gold, which suggests a flux doctrine far more radical than most people would admit. And in the course of this passage, he says, first, that it would be wrong to regard the sensible world as having some degree of stability (ὥς τινα ἔχον βεβαιότητα, 49d7), and in the course of the analogy between the sensible world and molten gold, that we cannot call the gold by the name of the shapes it assumes, because μεταξὺ τιθεμένου μεταπίπτει (50b3-4).

Now the detailed exegesis of this passage in general, and of the gold analogy in particular, has given rise to much scholarly debate. But I believe that the points I want to make about this passage are in fact relatively clear and uncontroversial. It is, I believe, clearly demonstrable that Plato is not here taking the view that everything is always in extreme flux. For, in the first place, Plato's goal in this section is to establish that there is a certain and secure answer to the question 'what is it?', when it is asked about the sensible world or about molten gold – 'it is *toiouton*', in the case of the sensible world, 'it is gold', in the case of the molten gold. And this fact is already sufficient to set apart the theory Plato is discussing here from the rampant flux theory canvassed in the *Theaetetus*. And then, if we pay careful attention to how Plato introduces this section, we learn that we are in fact being taught here only what can 'most safely by far' (49d3 cf 50b1) be said, and not what can be said *tout court*. To say that the stuff in the *Timaeus*, like molten gold, can only safely be called *toiouton*, in the same way as the gold can only safely be called gold, is not to say that it cannot be otherwise described. And if we ask 'what is it?', we *can* give an answer to it that is not the safe answer. Let us consider the transformations of our stuff in the *Timaeus* into water, cloud, ice, fire and so on (49bc). There is no problem here of the stuff's not being one or other of the set water, ice, cloud, fire and so on; it is just that we do not *know* which of them it is at any given time. We could commit ourselves by saying 'it's this' or 'it's that' – and we could either be right or wrong. Our answer would not be a safe answer. If we want to be safe, and we always want to be right, we should not commit ourselves, and should rest content with saying 'it's this kind of stuff'. Here, too, then, the text suggests that Plato did not believe in a rampant theory of flux, and that he did not think such a theory necessary for the argument for the theory of Forms that he mounts in 50d.

But if the text suggests that Plato did not defend the claim that there is no knowledge of the sensible world with a theory of rampant flux in the sensible world, it does not, on the other hand, tell us how Plato *did* defend this surprising claim. If we are to explain how Plato thought that normal constant change in the world supports the claim that the world cannot be known, we must turn to the argument for the theory of Forms in the *Republic*. The argument there is not exactly the same as the argument from flux as reported by Aristotle in the *Metaphysics* and as represented by Plato in the *Timaeus*. But whether or not the argument there is similar enough to the argument reported by Aristotle for us to be justified in calling it the argument from flux, it is certainly exactly structurally analogous with that argument. In particular, it too depends on the claim that the sensible world cannot be known. And even though, as we shall see, Plato does not there support this claim by reference to the view that the sensible world is continually changing, an examination of the argument in the *Republic* does, I think, nevertheless throw some light on the lacuna we have found in the argument in the *Timaeus*. And at the same time, such a study of *Republic* V will, I believe, substantiate my initial contention that the argument for the theory of Forms from flux depends on the same misunderstanding of the relation of context to contradiction that we witnessed in chapter 2.

The Argument in the Republic

If we have the direction of Plato's inference aright – if, that is, Plato tends to infer ontological conclusions from epistemological premisses – then we can expect to find, with Ross, the same ontological distinction between the sensible world and the world of Forms that we have seen in the *Timaeus*, when Plato introduces the same epistemological distinction, between knowledge and belief, in the *Republic*. For it is agreed on both sides of the dispute about the dating of the *Timaeus* that the doctrines advanced in the *Timaeus* are very similar to those of the *Republic*.

Some commentators, though, such as Annas, think that the line of argument for the theory of Forms in the *Republic* is 'in fact quite different from the flux argument' (p.153). The argument from flux is concerned with the *succession* of opposites, Annas says, but the argument in *Republic* V is concerned with the *compresence* of opposites. She believes that the best we can say for Aristotle is that he may have 'carelessly assimilated' the two arguments.[17] In this, of course, she echoes Owen, whose argument from compresent opposites she finds in *Republic* V. Owen believes that Plato himself 'took small care and had small motive to distinguish sharply, or to reconcile' an argument for the theory of Forms from incomplete predicates, and 'an extension of that argument to cover physical mutability'.[18] But we have found that the argument in the *Timaeus* corresponds to Aristotle's reconstruction of the argument from flux, and not to Owen's extension of the argument he finds for the theory of Forms from the compresence of opposites to cover physical mutability. So let us now examine the argument in *Republic* V, and see which pattern it follows.

I shall try first to show then, that the argument for the theory of Forms that we find in the *Republic* follows, in general outline, the argument for the theory of Forms from flux; and then turn to the defence that I think Plato makes here of the claim that the sensible world cannot be known, and argue that this defence shows us how to fill the lacuna in the argument from flux as we have found it in the *Timaeus*. At the same time, I hope to demonstrate that this defence rests on a misunderstanding of the relation of context to contradiction.

The argument in *Republic* V gets under way, as Murphy and Gosling have noted, in 476de, with the sightlover's imagined objection to proceedings.[19] The sightlover lays claim to knowledge; and Socrates here undertakes to show that he is wrong; that he has belief, and not knowledge, and that knowledge is reserved for the philosopher. He proceeds by claiming that there is a correlation between knowledge and the Forms, and between belief and the sensible world, and that for this reason, the philosopher, who alone has acquaintance with the Forms, alone has knowledge, while the sightlover, who has acquaintance only with the sensible world, has mere belief. The argument in *Republic* V is not, then, primarily a defence of the claim that there are such things as Forms. But Plato does have occasion to make some defence of this claim in the course of his argument against the sightlover – a defence that I shall argue runs along the same lines as the argument for the existence of Forms in the *Timaeus*.

The arguments fall into two main sections. In the first of these (467e7-478e6),

Plato argues, on largely epistemological grounds, that what we can know is *to on*, 'what is being', or *to pantelos on*, 'what is in every way being', whilst what we can believe is *to on kai me on*, 'what is both being and notbeing'. In the second section (478e7-479d5), Plato then gives us independent reasons that are not epistemological in character, for describing the sensible world as both being and notbeing, and Forms as just being, or as 'in every way being'. He is then, he thinks, in a position to conclude that the sightlover, who does not admit the existence of Forms, has belief and not knowledge (479d7-479e6) and that the philosopher, who admits the existence of Forms, alone has knowledge (479e7-8). We can thus represent Plato's general strategy in this argument as follows: he first claims that what can be known and what can be believed must satisfy certain conditions; and he subsequently argues that the sensible world satisfies the condition for being the object of belief, while the Forms satisfy the condition for being the object of knowledge. The defence of the theory of Forms embedded in this argument is that if there is knowledge, then there are objects that satisfy the conditions for being the objects of knowledge – viz Forms.[20]

Now if this general account of the argument is the right one, it is clear that Plato is indeed employing the same line of argument for the theory of Forms in *Republic* V that we find in the *Timaeus*. The argument, as I have set it out, moves from epistemological premises to ontological conclusions *via* the claim – here, for once, defended in some detail – that there is no knowledge of the physical world. And as ever, Plato simply assumes that objects that satisfy the conditions for being known, are Forms.

So let us now examine the argument in *Republic* V more closely, and see whether my general account of it is indeed the right one, and how Plato *does* here defend the view that there is no knowledge of the sensible world. I shall focus on the role that we should ascribe to contradiction in this argument; for, as I have already indicated, it will be my contention that Plato's view that there is no knowledge of the sensible world, and his consequent appeal to Forms, rests on the same view of the relation of context to contradiction that we witnessed in chapter 2.

Let us first consider the first section of the argument, and the connection Plato draws there between belief and 'what is being and notbeing'.

Belief, 'Being', and Contradiction

Socrates' first move in the argument is to establish a number of points of agreement with his interlocutors in epistemology – that what is in every way being is in every way knowable, that what is notbeing is not knowable in any way (477a3-4), that what is both being and notbeing lies between these two (what is truly being, and what is in no way being) (477a6-7), and that anything that lay between knowledge and *agnoia* would be *of* something that lies between what is truly being and what is in no way being (477a9-b1); that there is such a thing as belief (477b3), and that it is a different *dynamis* from knowledge (477b6-7). Plato seems to regard all these points as completely uncontroversial.

He then, in 477cd, gains Glaucon's assent to some remarks about *dynameis*, from which it follows that the same thing cannot be both believed and known (478a10-b2); and he argues next that belief is not, as *agnoia* is, directed at nothing (478b3-c6); that it falls between knowledge and *agnoia* in clarity, and so is of what is both being and notbeing, while knowledge is of what is truly being and *agnoia* is of what is notbeing (conclusion at 478e1-5).

Now there are numerous well-known problems about the detailed analysis of the argument here; but not all of these problems need concern us. I shall in fact, focus on just one disputed question – namely the sense of 'is' involved, and the implications of this for the meaning of the phrase 'what is being and notbeing'. For it is through this phrase, that Plato links belief with the sensible world.

At least three different views about the sense of 'is' here gain some support from the text – the traditional view, that the existential sense is in play here, is supported by Plato's remarks about *agnoia* in 478b3-c6; the view that Plato has the predicative sense in mind is supported by his use of the phrases 'what is being' and so on, in the second main section of the argument (which we have not as yet considered); while it is, as we shall see, perhaps most plausible to suppose, with Gosling and Fine, that the being and notbeing mentioned in the first section of the argument here, is veridical being and notbeing. (I shall follow Fine's practice hereafter, of referring to these senses of the verb 'is' as 'is-e', 'is-p' and 'is-v', respectively.)

There are two main reasons why it is attractive to take the being and notbeing here as veridical being and notbeing, and belief as correlated with what both is, and is not true. The first is, that, as Gosling notes, the argument is designed to convince a sightlover; and so we should take *to on* in the phrase *gignoskein to on* veridically; for the natural meaning of this phrase is 'to know the truth', or 'what is the case'.[21] The other merit of the position is that Plato offers little by way of argument for the view that belief is of what is being and notbeing – and this suggestion enables us to see the point Plato is making here as uncontentious, and not in need of serious argument. His point is simply that some beliefs are true, while other beliefs are false. (It is natural to take 'belief' here to refer to the class of beliefs, and not to individual beliefs. There are two reasons for this. One is that Plato says at 477a6-7 that belief is fallible, while knowledge is infallible; and this suggests that he thinks 'belief' sometimes errs and sometimes does not. And secondly, it is reasonable to suppose that an individual true belief will resemble knowledge, and will be correlated with what is being, while an individual false belief will resemble *agnoia*, and will be correlated with what is in no way being. In order to find a combination of what is being with what is notbeing, we must, it seems, consider the class of beliefs, and not individual beliefs).

Now let us consider how the case stands, if Plato is indeed employing is-v here, and belief is correlated with what is and is not *true*. In this case, the being in question here will be incompatible with the notbeing in question here, in so far as true propositions are incompatible with false ones. Not that all true propositions are incompatible with all false propositions, of course; but that there is always a true proposition *p*, that is incompatible with each false proposition not-*p*, and *vice versa*. And so there is at least the possibility of incompatibility between the being and the notbeing with which belief is correlated – if, that is, the being here is veridical being.

But, as I have just mentioned, there is evidence that Plato does not consistently employ is-v in this passage. In 478b3-c6, when Plato is arguing that belief is not, like *agnoia*, correlated with what is not-being, he seems to employ is-e and not is-v. He seems here to identify 'what is notbeing', *to me on*, with 'nothing', *meden* (478b12-c1); and it is natural to take this as 'nothing that exists', and to suppose that is-e is in play here. Then again, *agnoia* will, in the last analysis, be correlated neither with Forms, nor with sensible things; and this too suggests that Plato is now using is-e. Finally, the argument at this point bears a marked resemblance to arguments we find in *Theaetetus* 189, and *Sophist* 237; and in those arguments, it is also natural to suppose that Plato is employing is-e. And though Plato may very well have seen a connection between the existential and the predicative uses of *einai*, is-e and is-p, it is hard to find any connection between the existential and veridical uses, is-e and is-v.[22]

Then again, in the second part of the argument, as we shall see (below pp.61-63), Plato identifies the 'being' in question, when we know *to on*, with the 'being' that he thinks to characterize Forms, and he identifies the 'being and notbeing' that is correlative to belief, with the 'being and notbeing' that he thinks to characterize particulars. The being of Forms, and the being and notbeing of particulars, however, is not veridical, but predicative being (and notbeing). Plato's claim is not that Forms are true, and particulars both true and false – the predicates 'true' and 'false' do not properly apply to Forms and particulars. His claim in 479 is that with respect to some predicate F, particulars both are and are not (F), but Forms can be truly said to be (F). So Fine, who accepts Gosling's view that 'is' in this argument is initially used in the veridical sense, but who admits that the 'is' of 479 is the predicative 'is', has seen the possible options here very clearly. She writes as follows: 'does Plato simply confuse is-v and is-p? Or is there a plausible connecting link between the two uses of "esti"?' (p.135).

Perhaps the most plausible suggestion offered to date is that of Kahn, who claims that an equivalence between 'x is (really) F' and 'it is the case (that x is F)' may help Plato at this point.[23] This may be what Plato has in mind – though if so, it is to be regretted that he did not make his thinking explicit as this point.

Whether we accept Kahn's suggestion or not, however, it does not immediately help us much in understanding why Plato thinks that there is no knowledge of the sensible world. If we *are* to understand why Plato thought the sensible world to be correlated with belief rather than knowledge, we must, I believe, turn to the second part of the argument, and see why Plato thinks that the sensible world, like our beliefs about it, is to be described as 'both being and not being'.

The Sensible World, 'Being' and Contradiction

The second main section of the argument is comparatively straightforward. Socrates simply gains agreement from Glaucon that each of the many beautifuls, and so on, will appear the opposite – and so, will both *be* and *not be* (beautiful, and so on) (479a5-b10).[24] He does not here tell us why he thinks that this is so. It is reasonable, then, to suppose that he is making the familiar point that things appear different in different contexts.[25]

Now if this is the reason why Plato thinks that the sensible world, like our beliefs about it, is to be called 'both being and notbeing', it raises the question whether the argument in *Republic* V really does resemble the argument in the *Timaeus* as closely as I claim. In both the *Republic* and the *Timaeus* Plato expresses the strange view that we are trying to account for, that belief is related to the sensible world, while knowledge is related to Forms. But while in the *Timaeus*, Plato refers at this point to the fact that the sensible world is in a state of continuous change, in the *Republic*, he suggests that there is no knowledge of the sensible world because it can be described as being and notbeing. This, no doubt, is why commentators such as Annas see a different argument for the theory of Forms in *Republic* V from that advanced in the *Timaeus*.

Now my primary claim against Annas (and against Owen), is that she disregards the structure of the argument in *Republic* V, and so fails to see that it is identical to the structure of the argument in the *Timaeus*. It might seem, however, that whatever the structure of the two arguments, the substantive difference between them alone would prevent us from associating the argument in the *Republic* with the argument from flux in the *Timaeus*. I shall argue now, however, that the two texts are more closely related in this respect than they seem to be; and that we can see how in the *Timaeus* Plato might think that the physical world can be described as both being and notbeing, and how considerations of flux enter into the argument in *Republic* V.

Let us turn first to the *Republic*, then. Now the text of *Republic* V may initially seem to support Annas' contention that Plato is concerned here with compresence, and not succession, of opposites. For we have seen that in the second main section of the argument, Plato does not mention change in the world, when he says that each of the many beautifuls and so on, will also appear the opposite. And when he is discussing the correlates of knowledge and belief in the first section of the argument, he seems to emphasize, at 478d5-6, that the opposites that interest him are not successive, but compresent. Just as knowledge corresponds to the εἰλικρινῶς ὄν, and *agnoia* to the πάντως μὴ ὄν, so belief is related to the ἅμα ὄν τε καὶ μὴ ὄν (note, with Owen, the ἅμα).[26]

But considerations of flux are not as alien to this context as they may at first appear. This becomes clear, once we see, with Murphy and Gosling, that the contrast Plato is drawing here is not necessarily that between particular and universal, but may be that between token and type. We cannot find the compresence of opposed predicates in some of the examples here, unless we consider types, rather than tokens. This becomes especially clear, if we turn to *Republic* VI, with Gosling.[27] There, in 538cd, Plato examines the case of *ta dikaia*. *Republic* I illustrates what is in question: the type-action, repaying debts, is sometimes just and sometimes unjust, though its tokens may be unqualifiedly just or unqualifiedly unjust. The type is both being and notbeing just, but the tokens need not admit of the compresence of just and unjust at all.

Now we need not claim, as Gosling does, that all the examples quoted in *Republic* V are to be understood in the same way, after this model. As F. C. White has recently pointed out, the case of 'double', which Plato cites, is particularly hard to construe in this fashion.[28] And he makes the further sound point that elsewhere (namely in the *Symposium*), Plato shows us many different ways in which particular beautifuls both are, and are not, beautiful, any or all of which may apply to any, or all, of the examples cited in *Republic* V.[29] My point is simply, that once we have seen that Plato is not exclusively concerned with the compresence of opposites in a given particular at a given time, the concept of change through time will no longer seem irrelevant to Plato's point about being and notbeing. Change through time will be one of a number of reasons we might give for saying that particulars are both being and notbeing.[30]

We are now in a position, then, to make good the lacuna we found in the argument for the theory of Forms in the *Timaeus*. At least, we can now see how what Plato says about being and notbeing in the *Republic*, can be applied to the various transformations of the stuff in the *Timaeus* (even if we cannot as yet see why 'what is both being and notbeing' cannot be known). At any given time, a specimen of the stuff will be e.g. fire. But at another time, the same stuff will not be what it was before, but will be something else (i.e. another one of its possible manifestations). And we can draw together these two temporally different manifestations of the stuff, and say that it both *is*, and *is not* fire, for example. Similarly, we can draw together various token actions of the same type, and say that the type-action, repaying debts, for examples, both *is* and *is not* just. It may be just to return a friend's knife until the friend goes mad – and it may be possible to locate the onset of his madness exactly in time. But it is still one and the same (type-) act that both *is* and *is not* just, and one and the same stuff that both *is* and *is not* fire. So perhaps it is not unduly paradoxical to consider the type-action, repaying debts apart from its tokens, and say of it that it both is and is not just at the same time; or even, similarly, to consider our stuff apart from its temporal context, and say of it just that it is stuff, or that it both is and is not e.g. fire at the same time.[31]

We have now seen how Plato might have applied what he says about the being and notbeing of the sensible world in the *Republic* to the sensible world as it figures in the *Timaeus*. But we have not as yet seen why Plato should have thought that his remarks about being and notbeing show that there is no knowledge of the sensible world. We have, however, seen that when Plato says that the sensible world is both being and notbeing, he seems to have much the same sort of thing in mind as he does when he complains about the senses' reports on the sensible world. And when we examined those complaints in chapter 2, we saw that he seemed to suffer from a misunderstanding of the relation of context to contradiction. It is reasonable to conjecture, then, that he may have made the same sort of mistake here. The simplest possible hypothesis would be that Plato thought that there could be no knowledge of the sensible world, because he thought it self-contradictory; and there can be no knowledge of self-contradictory entities. I shall argue later that we must in fact adopt a more complicated view of the matter. But as this simple hypothesis would give a good account of why Plato thought that there was no knowledge of the sensible world, let us first examine it in more detail, and then consider possible objections to it, and modify our view accordingly.

Context, Contradiction and Flux

In chapter 2, we saw how Plato's misunderstanding of the relation of context to contradiction leads Plato to face an unreal logical difficulty of apparent contradiction. In this chapter, my suggestion is, that the same misunderstanding leads him to face an unreal epistemological difficulty. The only difference will be, that whereas in chapter 2, we saw Plato puzzled by difference of relation, here his difficulties will be caused by difference in time. That a thing has different, and incompatible, properties in different relations, or at different times, seems to us to show that it is not a self-contradictory item. But for Plato, I would argue that the reverse is true. He sees clearly that differences of physical, or temporal, context, are what enable us to form propositions that attribute incompatible properties to one and the same thing. But he does not see that these very differences of context render a thing's possession of such incompatible attributes non-contradictory.

The contradictions of the sensible world would – on the simple hypothesis we are considering – lead Plato to think that knowledge of it is impossible. None the less (for reason or reasons unknown), he remains convinced that knowledge is possible. So he has a difficulty here – to which, in this chapter, we will have seen two different possible resolutions.

One resolution is that tried and rejected in the *Theaetetus*. There the objects of knowledge exist only fleetingly, at one instant in time. No two propositions concern one and the same thing; and so, *a fortiori*, no two propositions ascribe apparently incompatible properties to one and the same thing. And so, in the world of *Theaetetus* 152-160, knowledge, and perceptual knowledge at that, would be possible.

The other possible resolution of Plato's difficulty is that represented by the theory of Forms. In the world of Forms, knowledge is possible because Forms never change; they are always the same as themselves, and at no instant are they self-contradictory. And so here, too, we can never draw together two potentially contradictory propositions. A theory of rampant flux in the world, and the theory of Forms, then, represent, for Plato, opposite routes to one and the same goal, that of escape from the difficulties of the relation of temporal context to contradiction.[32]

These two possible resolutions of Plato's problem here may instructively be compared with the two possible resolutions we saw in chapter 2, of the logical difficulty that Plato finds in one and the same object's having opposed attributes in different relations. One resolution of that problem, I suggested there, was to specify very exactly what bears the predicates in question, and to say that they are in fact borne by different logical parts of the thing in question. And this resolution of the logical difficulty parallels the resolution of the epistemological difficulty provided by the world of the *Theaetetus*. For there, two opposed predicates are never borne by one and the same thing, but always by two completely non-identical entities. In both cases, new and unusually strong conditions of identity enable us to identify entities, 'logical' parts of particulars, or objects tht exist only for an instant, that are immune from the vagaries of context. Plato's other resolution to the logical difficulty, advanced in *Parmenides* 129, consists in a retreat to the world of Forms, where there are no difficulties of context and contradiction. And this, of course, is the same as the resolution Plato favours of his epistemological problem. In this case, a whole world is posited, that is free from temporal context.

I suggested in chapter 2 (see p.32 above) that the Platonic contrast between *kath' hauto* and *pros heteron* is very naturally employed in sceptical arguments. And now that epistemology, and not logic, is in question, the point of the comparison becomes very evident. Both Plato and the sceptics deny that there is knowledge of the sensible world; and both ground their position on the same evidence. The Platonic and the sceptical philosopher alike point to the fact that things have different and opposed predicates true of them, when we consider them not in themselves, but in relation to their environment. The sceptic then says that we cannot know which of these opposed predicates that seem to be true of a thing really are true of it: things have an equal claim to be called both 'F' and 'not-F', and so cannot be known to be either. Plato, by contrast, seeks to advance his case, by saying that things both are and are not 'F'. And from this, he concludes that they are objects of belief, and not knowledge. Both arguments alike, then, depend on our believing that we cannot know that an item in the world both is and is not (some predicate).

That, then, is an account of how we can explain Plato's reluctance to believe that there can be knowledge of the sensible world, if we accept the simple hypothesis that Plato was led by his mistakes about the relation of context to contradiction to think the sensible world irretrievably self-contradictory.

But we saw in chapter 2, in our discussion of Plato and the law of contradiction (pp.35-41 above), that Plato does not ultimately seem to think the world self-contradictory. He seems inclined to admit, as we all do, that it is *possible* for different, and incompatible predicates to hold true of the same thing at different times, in different respects and so on; and so, that it is not contradictory. Plato's shortcoming on this count, proved to be simply that he did not understand the real reason *why* such states of affairs are not in fact contradictory.

So let us ask now, whether, if Plato did *not* think the sensible world self-contradictory after all, but simply failed to understand why it is not self-contradictory, this would still enable us to explain why Plato thought that there was no knowledge of the sensible world.

I believe it is clear that it could not do so. But perhaps Aristotle is somewhat astray after all, and Plato did not hold quite that there is no knowledge of the sensible world – but just, that there is no knowledge of the sensible world for the non-philosopher. After all, we saw, in chapter 2 how the theory of Forms enabled Plato to maintain that the intellect is ultimately able to construe the senses' reports on the physical world in an uncontradictory fashion. In epistemology too, perhaps, Plato is reluctant to deprive the philosopher of knowledge of the sensible world.

As Fine has emphasized (p.121), Plato distinctly says at *Republic* 520, that the philosopher who returns to the cave will have knowledge of the things there: συνεθιζόμενοι γὰρ μυρίῳ βέλτιον ὄψεσθε τῶν ἐκεῖ καὶ γνώσεσθε ἕκαστα τὰ εἴδωλα ἅττα ἐστι καὶ ὧν (520c3-5). And this can hardly be a mere slip of Plato's pen. For the philosopher-guardian of the *Republic*, who is to rule the ideal state, will surely make knowledgeable decisions about the sensible world. Perhaps, then, we should conclude, not that Plato thought the sensible world irretrievably contradictory; but simply that this is how he thought it must seem to the non-philosopher, who does not have knowledge of the Forms.

It is worth expanding on this point a little. My suggestion is, basically, that the sightlover has belief about the sensible world, because he cannot explain why the sensible world is not contradictory. The philosopher, on the other hand, has knowledge of the sensible world, because he can explain why it is uncontradictory. And this state of affairs comes about simply because Forms exist, and the philosopher has knowledge of them. And to the question, why the sightlover cannot resolve the apparent contradictions in the same way as the philosopher, the answer is that if he *does* think of doing so, then his intellect has been awoken, and he is already on the way to becoming a philosopher himself.

The point is, that Plato would not himself go about disarming the apparent contradictions of the sensible world as we would today; and so this method of dealing with these apparent contradictions is not available either to the sightlover or to the philosopher. The sightlover is left without a method of resolving these apparent contradictions. But the philosopher's knowledge of the Forms gives him the power to discriminate the F from the not-F characteristics of sensible things – he will posit the existence of logical parts that exist in particulars at given times. He will deal in pure, unmixed entities that will not block his route to knowledge by giving rise to apparent contradictions. And so, the sightlover will have at best belief about the sensible world, while for the philosopher, the route to knowledge will be clear.

Conclusion

I remarked earlier, that the view that there is no knowledge of the sensible world has seemed to commentators to argue a strange view, either of knowledge, or of the sensible world. I have argued, by contrast, that we need attribute to Plato only the view that there is no knowledge of the sensible world, if there are no Forms, and no knowledge of Forms; and further, that we can understand this view, if we attribute to Plato the same misunderstanding of the relation of context to contradiction that we have met before, in chapter 2.

In chapter 4, we will once again see Plato presenting us with an argument for the theory of Forms that depends on his view of the relation of contradiction. Meanwhile, however, I would like to summarize my conclusions about the argument for the theory of Forms in *Republic* V. We are now in a position to see that the argument for the theory of Forms in the *Republic* is essentially analogous to the argument from flux set out in Aristotle's *Metaphysics* and in the *Timaeus*. It differs from that argument largely in being more fully worked out in some areas, and less fully worked out in others. In the *Republic*, Plato argues for the distinction between knowledge and belief, which is taken for granted in the *Timaeus*. The existence of knowledge, however, is still assumed. (Presumably, the sightlover of the *Republic* would assent to the premiss 'there is knowledge', since he lays claim to knowledge himself.) Plato still makes the claim that there is no knowledge of the sensible world. He does not back up this claim by an appeal to flux theory. But he does make some attempt to explicate his claim here – and his explication is as relevant to the argument from flux as it is to the argument he offers here. This explication consists, as we have seen, in saying that the objects of belief, and the sensible world can both alike be described as both being and notbeing. The conclusion remains constant: that there are entities, 'Forms', that are objects of knowledge, because they are not both being and notbeing, but always are just what they are. And in both cases, the argument turns on the same misunderstanding of the relation of context to contradiction that we examined in chapter 2.

A question I shall pose in chapter 5, is whether the Forms Plato derives here are the same as the Forms he derives from the argument deployed in *Parmenides* 129, and from the argument from explanation to which chapter 4 is devoted. I shall argue that the difficulty is not so great as Annas (quoted on p.48 above) suggests, in so far as all these arguments do depend on a common view of contradiction. First, however, I shall argue that Plato's argument for the theory of Forms from explanation does indeed depend on this self-same view of his about context and contradiction.

NOTES

1. *Aristotle's Metaphysics* 193.

2. Ross 193. Hardie also says that these two passages state 'arguments along similar lines' (13).

3. *Aristotle's Metaphysics Books M and N* 153.

4. This point is noticed by Fine, 'Knowledge and Belief in *Republic* V' 137 and n.22.

5. 'Plato's Distinction between Being and Becoming' 83.

6. 'A Proof in the *Peri Ideon*' 307-8.

7. Gosling, *Plato*, see esp. 156, 175 and 188; Vlastos, 'A Metaphysical Paradox' 54. For Vlastos, 'Plato recognizes only one kind of knowledge', 'Degrees Of Reality' 73.

8. Gosling, *Plato* 142.

9. On 'patterns of becoming', see Bolton 72-4.

10. Irwin's view is also set out briefly in his *Plato's Moral Theory*.

11. *Plato's Moral Theory* 148.

12. 'Plato's argument for Forms did not rely ... on s-change in the sensible world'. 'Plato's Heracliteanism' 12.

13. 'Plato's Heracliteanism' 6.

14. Cf. Bolton 74-6.

15. See 357 n.1.

16. Bolton's reconstruction of the argument has the advantage that it renders the argument valid; but it has the very considerable disadvantage that it requires us to read 'false belief' for 'belief' throughout (see 77, esp. n.24).

17. See Annas 153.

18. Owen, 'Proof' 308.

19. Gosling, '*Doxa* and *Dynamis* in Plato's *Republic*' 121; Murphy, *Plato's Republic* 105.

20. Fine (137 n.22) makes the point that we must supply the premiss 'there is knowledge' for the argument to be valid. She compares here not only *Timaeus* 51d, but also *Parmenides* 135ac. We may also compare *Phaedo* 74b2, where, as we saw in chapter 1, Socrates simply expects his interlocutor to agree that we have knowledge of the equal.

21. Gosling, '*Doxa* and *Dynamis*' 129. Fine (125) rightly makes the point that other interpretations violate the condition of uncontroversiality. Kahn prefers to translate is-v by 'is the case', rather than 'is true'; but nothing hangs on this for our present purposes.

22. Gosling, '*Doxa* and *Dynamis*' 127, regards this passage as simply confused. Fine's attempt to construe 'nothing' as 'nothing true' (131) is most implausible. It may indeed be the case, as she claims, that if I maintain that 'justice is a vegetable', this 'does not amount to a claim about justice at all; it displays total ignorance of justice'. But she has made no attempt to come to terms with what Plato says here about believing *one* thing and believing *no* thing. Yet this is one of the main reasons for supposing is-e in play here.

23. See Kahn 121.

24. This is the point in the argument at which Plato moves from talking about opposites (beautiful and its opposite, and so on) to talking about *being* and *notbeing* (beautiful and so on).

25. Thus Vlastos turns at this point to the *Symposium* for elucidation of this ('Degrees of Reality' 66).

26. Owen, 'Proof' 307 n.1. See too Murphy, esp. 110-1. Plato does, however, mention that Forms are unchanging at 479a2-3.

27. '*Republic* V: *Ta Polla Kala*' 125.

28. 'J. Gosling on *Ta Polla Kala*' 128.

29. See 129-30.

30. Moravesik writes 'temporal being is not complete being, what is temporal, both is and is not' (11). F. C. White, 'The *Phaedo* and *Republic* V on Essences' 154, inadvertently points to one reason why Plato may emphasize change through time. He points out that some particulars do hold some predicates essentially – and so, could presumably be known. In reply to this, Plato could simply say that these particulars do not exist forever.

31. We might want to say at this point, not that we now understand the argument from flux; but rather, that we see here how the argument picked out by Aristotle, and the arguments we have examined in the *Timaeus* and in *Republic* V, are continuous with the considerations we saw Plato advancing in chapter 2. But of course it does not matter what we say here, so long as we understand the facts under discussion.

32. I thus agree with Hintikka (*Time and Necessity*, ch.4) that the two views 'knowledge is perception' and 'knowledge is of the eternal', are 'really two sides of the same coin' (78). It should be noted, however, that Hintikka reaches this conclusion by a very different route from mine (*via* his view that for Plato, knowledge is a kind of mental vision).

4. THE ARGUMENT FROM EXPLANATION

Introduction

We saw at the start of chapter 3 that Aristotle says that two considerations led Plato to adopt the theory of Forms, one derived from Heraclitus, the other from Socrates. We have now considered the question of Heraclitus' influence on Plato, and Plato's argument for the theory of Forms from flux; in this chapter, I shall examine the influence of Socrates on Plato, and Plato's argument for the theory of Forms from explanation. I shall contend that we find an argument for the theory of Forms from explanation in a 'One Over Many' argument in the *Phaedo*, and that this argument once again demonstrates that Plato did not fully understand the relation of context to contradiction.

Aristotle's Evidence

Aristotle tells us in *Metaphysics* M that Plato believed in the separate existence of universals, whereas Socrates had not (1078b30-1). But to the question *why* Plato separated universals, when Socrates had not, Aristotle here gives us no answer. In *Metaphysics* A, however, he says that Plato's reason for positing the separate existence of universals was that he thought, with Heraclitus, that the sensible world is in flux, and so is not susceptible to definition. Thus the theory of Forms, on this account of it, arises from the simple application of Heraclitus' views about flux to Socrates' views about definition and universals. Aristotle here, then, presents us not with two, but just with one, argument for the theory of Forms.

Elsewhere, however, especially when criticising the theory of Forms, Aristotle does recognize an argument for the theory that has nothing at all to do with considerations of flux in the sensible world. This is the so-called 'One Over Many' argument for the existence of Forms; and it is this argument that I propose to examine in this chapter, and to relate to ideas about universals.

The One Over Many argument for the theory of Forms, together with the so-called 'Third Man Regress' (to which it is intimately related), is presented in the first part of the *Parmenides*. It is also, as is generally recognized, mentioned by Plato at *Republic* 596ab, where Socrates says εἶδος γάρ πού τι ἓν ἕκαστον εἰώθαμεν τίθεσθαι περὶ ἕκαστα τὰ πολλά, οἷς ταὐτὸν ὄνομα ἐπιφέρομεν (596a5-8) – though the precise interpretation of this passage is in dispute.[1] It was once thought that this was the sole reference to this argument for the theory of Forms in Plato's middle period. Thus Annas called this an argument that Plato casually mentions once, and claimed that Plato explicitly renounced it in the later period.[2] Gosling expressed the same general view, and at the same time gave a brief summary of the One Over Many argument in the following passage: 'there are ... only two places in which Plato seems to betray an interest in the argument that if there are many instances of F, then there must be something, F, to which they are all related in a way that justifies the use of a common term' (*Plato*, p.191 – Gosling has in mind *Republic* 596 and *Parmenides* 132). Fine has recently recognized, however, that Plato's interest in at least some restricted form of One Over Many principle dates backwards in time to the Socratic dialogues, and the interest expressed there in definitions, and that it reaches forward in time to the *Politicus*, where Plato does not so much give up the One Over Many principle, as guard against its misuse.[3] In this chapter, I shall focus on just one passage in which Plato shows an interest in a One Over Many principle of some sort, namely *Phaedo* 96ff., with a view to explaining how it is that this principle leads Plato to posit the existence of Forms, rather than to a theory of universals. I shall first give a brief account of the passage, and of the divergent views that commentators have taken about it. I shall then argue that we find here not just a form of One Over Many argument for the existence of Forms, but also a further manifestation of Plato's misunderstanding of the relation of context to contradiction. Finally, I shall seek confirmation for this account of the passage by relating the theory of explanation Plato expresses here, to Russell's theory of universals.

Phaedo *96ff.*

In *Phaedo* 96ff., Socrates outlines a number of difficulties in the theory of explanation. One reason he says he has for finding some explanations unsatisfactory is that they are not teleological in character. But although he makes much of this complaint it has, I think, been demonstrated by Vlastos, that he makes no attempt to resolve the difficulties he finds in this area. As Vlastos has pointed out, Plato says clearly in 99cd that he cannot resolve these difficulties.[4]

But there is also another sort of difficulty that Socrates thinks to be presented by some of our ordinary explanations, and one that he plainly thinks can be resolved – if, that is, we accept the hypothesis that there are Forms.

So, as the theory of Forms is our primary concern here, let us focus our attention on those cases Socrates presents here that may initially puzzle the philosopher, but that he later resolves to his satisfaction with the help of the theory of Forms. This means, in fact, concentrating on the set of problems first mentioned in 96d8-97b8, and subsequently taken up and resolved in 100e8-101c9.

In the first of these two passages, Socrates considers at length just one of the examples he mentions, namely the explanation of the coming into being of two (*he aitia* ... *tou duo genesthai*, 97a4-5). Socrates here rejects two explanations of this phenomenon, 'addition' and 'division'. He rejects 'addition' as a possible explanation of this, on the grounds that it is not clear *what* has become two – whether it is one or other of the units that are added together, or whether it is both of them (96e6-97a1). And he further comments about this that he does not see how their being placed together can make the units become two, when both the units in question were one before (97a3). And Socrates rejects 'division', the other potential explanation of the coming into being of two, with the remark that 'it becomes opposed to the former explanation of the coming into being of two' (97a7-b1) – that is, 'addition'.

Now after his discussion of this example, Socrates moves off to discuss his interest in teleology (97b8ff.). But is seems clear from the text here that the examples Socrates has referred to immediately before this (those involving big and small, ten and eight, and two and one cubit) are all to be understood in much the same way. And this is confirmed later, in 100e8-101c9, where Socrates resolves all these problems employing the hypothesis that there are Forms.[5] And there is a suggestion in this later passage, that opposition lies at the heart of his complaint about our ordinary explanations of these phenomena. For he objects here that the explanation we might be tempted to give of A's being bigger than B, 'by a head' (whatever this means), gives rise to an 'opposed account' (*enantios logos*) of the matter (101a5-7).

Now it is evidently by no means easy to detect the precise nature of the problem Socrates finds in our ordinary explanations here: Socrates himself had once accepted such explanations without question – and Cebes at the time of the dialogue still finds them perfectly satisfactory (see 96e5). Moreover, there is still dispute among commentators today as to where the difficulty is supposed to lie, and what is supposed to cause it. So let us now examine some of the views taken about this question.

Let us turn first to Vlastos. Vlastos has suggested, in his 'Reasons and Causes in the *Phaedo*', that here as elsewhere (on his view) Plato is trying to distinguish physical contingency from logical necessity. Thus the puzzles of 96d-97b 'arise because physical factors are being confused with logical ones' (p.99, n.61). Socrates' original problem was that 'he was assuming that a material factor ... could account for ... statements, all of which are *a priori*, and could only be accounted for by referring to the meaning of the terms they use' (p.99).[6] The hypothesis that there are Forms provides a suitable – because logically necessary – account of such *a priori* propositions. To the criticism that some of the examples Plato mentions do not seem, in fact, to involve logical necessity, Vlastos responds that we must recognize Plato's 'firm conviction that all intelligible necessity ... must be grounded on logical necessity, since it represents the inter-relations of eternal Forms' (p.110).

Now Vlastos' view is impressively coherent. But it does not, I think, reflect the nature of Plato's problems, or his solution of them, very accurately. Vlastos freely admits that the first four puzzles Plato presents us with in the passage under consideration are 'peculiarly mystifying to the modern reader' (p.95). Of all the explanations Plato rejects as unsatisfactory, Vlastos believes that in only one – the case in which Plato rejects 'addition' as the explanation of the coming into being of two – is it immediately obvious what is wrong with the explanation. Vlastos suggests that in this case, Socrates 'had been confusing the arithmetical operation of addition with a physical process' (p.97). Certainly, as Vlastos goes on to claim in support of this interpretation, Plato's remarks in 97a2-5 can naturally be read in this manner. 'Which of the two original units is it that becomes two?' is certainly a strange question; and it may be Plato's point that it is a strange question. But when Vlastos goes on to claim (as he must) that the other puzzles do, in fact, follow the same pattern as this one, his view becomes much less plausible. What is wrong with Vlastos' interpretation here, is that it neglects Plato's emphasis on opposition. Vlastos does mention this (see note 57 on p.97), correctly diagnosing Plato's idea that there is a problem here because 'division' and 'addition' are opposed, as a fallacy. Nonetheless, fallacious though it may be, Plato does mention this supposed problem with our ordinary explanations at this point, and as we have seen, he returns to the idea of opposition later, in his discussion of the two men who differ in height by a head.

Vlastos' account of Plato's problems with our ordinary explanations is thus at odds with Plato's chosen emphasis. And so too, I believe, is his account of Plato's resolution of those problems. The 'clever' explanations admitted later in the dialogue are a fair mixture of different sorts of explanation. They may indeed all be necessary in some sense; but they are certainly not all logical in character. (For a discussion of 'clever' explanations, see p.78 below.) And it is surely most implausible to hold, as Vlastos does, that Plato thought that these explanations must manifest a deep similarity in kind, even though they appear so diverse. There is no indication whatever in the text that Plato thinks his examples of 'clever' explanations are all of one kind, or that he is talking here of 'physical laws that have logical necessity' as Vlastos claims (p.105).[7]

Other commentators have suggested that the interest Plato shows in explanation here is linked in some way with his interest in context-dependent predicates, or with his interest in flux. Now I shall argue in due course that there is indeed a link between Plato's ideas on these three topics. And this is, after all, what we would expect, given that all three topics alike are linked with the theory of Forms. But I would like, first, to demonstrate that the problems that face Plato are not themselves identical with one another.

Let us first compare the problem Plato finds here with the problem posed for him by flux. In chapter 3, we saw that Plato was troubled by the fact that one and the same individual can apparently have different, and opposed, properties at different points in time. What is water today may be fire tomorrow, for instance. Now some of the examples Plato mentions in *Phaedo* 96ff. also involve change in the world. For example, when we add two units to form two, it is plausible to claim that the various particulars involved in this transformation enjoy different, and incompatible, properties at different times. But it is not this aspect of the event, of course, that Plato asks us to consider, but the opposed explanations, 'addition' and 'division'. And not all the cases Plato mentions *do* involve change in the world: the case of the two men who differ in height by a head does not involve change in the world. We may conclude, then, that Plato's problem here is not to be identified with his problem concerning change in the world.

Let us now turn to the question whether this passage simply presents us with a further specimen of Plato's interest in 'incomplete' predicates. Gosling has suggested that 'it is in fact an important feature of the predicates concerned that they are incomplete. No object can be fine without being a fine such-and-such, nor equal without being equal to A or B'.[8] The examples we are invited to consider in this passage, however, are by no means identical with those we examined in chapter 2. A typical example of a problem with a context dependent predicate is that of a man who is big in one context, and small in another context. The case of the coming into being of two is, of course, far removed from such an example; for in none of the particulars concerned in that case do we find at any moment a compresence of opposed properties. The example of the two men who differ in height by a head does not fit the pattern we saw established in chapter 2 either. For here too, the opposition we are invited to consider does not lie in one or other of the two particular men – neither is (nor could be) described as being both bigger and smaller (that would take three people) – but in the explanation 'by a head'.

We have seen, then, that Plato is not here trying to distinguish the *a priori* from the *a posteriori* in explanation; and that he is not simply troubled here by his problems over flux or context dependent predicates. But we have not yet seen why Plato *is* troubled by the explanations he rejects here. After all, we ourselves are quite happy to say with Cebes that 'addition' and 'division', opposed though they are, can both be explanations of the coming into being of two – on different occasions, and in different circumstance, that is. And we are also content to join the youthful Socrates in holding that A can be bigger than B by a head, and B smaller than A by a head, without finding the 'opposition' involved in this account at all troubling.

Context, Contradiction and Explanation

But it is not hard, I believe, once we have formulated the matter in this way, to see what is going wrong here. This is, that Plato is once again misunderstanding the relevance of context here, just as he does in his discussions of compresent opposites, and flux. More formally, the idea that Plato is lacking here may be that of a causal field, as it is expounded by J. L. Mackie in his article, 'Causes and Conditions'.[9] Mackie believes that statements of the form 'A caused P' are usually elliptical, and are to be expanded into 'A caused P in relation to field F'. Thus, if we ask what causes influenza, we may mean, 'why do some people catch the virus, and others not?'; but then again, we might mean 'given that influenza viruses are present, why do some people contract the disease when others do not?'.[10] In the first case, the field in question is human beings in general, but in the second, it is human beings in conditions where influenza viruses are present. Thus, the question 'what causes influenza?' is partially incomplete and indeterminate.

Now Mackie here is interested in causal explanations alone. But much the same point is made by von Fraasen in his article 'The Pragmatics of Explanation' with regard to non-causal forms of explanation. Indeed, von Fraasen makes the plausible claim that context can determine what sort of explanation we deem appropriate. Thus he cites an example in which 'the question why the porch light is on may be answered "because I flipped the light switch" or "because we are expecting company"' (p.149).

Now if we apply this sort of analysis to Plato's problems in the *Phaedo*, we can see that they arise because Plato misunderstands the relation of context to contradiction. In this case, we find that he ignores the relevant causal fields. Plato asks the question, 'what causes the coming into being of two?'. The question is in fact partially incomplete and indeterminate. We are not in fact asking the same question, and so we do not expect the same answer, when we start with two units (let us call them D and E), and add them, and when we start with one unit (let us call if F), and divide it. Plato, however, treats the two questions as though they were one and the same; and so he expects the same answer – or at least compatible answers – to them. Thus the problem arises for Plato at precisely the point at which for us it is resolved. Plato does acknowledge and exploit the fact that different causal fields are involved when he sets up the problem – we do have to start with D and E in the one case, and F in the other, in order to produce incompatible answers to what seems to be the same question ('what is the explanation of the coming into being of two?'). In just the same way, we saw in chapter 2, that Plato did not understand the true significance of context when discussing the apparent contradiction that arises from the use of context-dependent predicates; but that he did see, and exploit the fact that different contexts are involved. And in chapter 3, we saw that Plato was inclined to think the sensible world contradictory because sensible particulars enjoy incompatible properties at different times. This once again involves recognition that different (temporal) contexts are an essential feature of the apparent contradiction under discussion, but a failure to appreciate their true significance.

The case of the two men and the head is closely analogous to the case of the coming into being of two. As in the first sort of contradiction, Plato here expects either just one, or at least compatible explanations of being small. So far, then, this case is exactly parallel to the first case. But then Plato notices that being big is incompatible with being small; and so he expects any explanation of being big to be incompatible with any explanation of being small. What is wrong with the explanation 'by a head', then, is that it is used to explain both being big, and being small. If Plato had recognized the importance of the incomplete and indeterminate nature of the questions 'why are things big/bigger?' and 'why are things small/smaller?', then he would not have found it problematic that one and the same thing can account for A's being big, in relation to certain circumstances, and B's being small, in relation to other circumstances.[11]

(In this example, Plato also takes one state of affairs – the relation of A to B in height – for two – A's being smaller than B's being bigger. On the reading I have just given of the contradiction involved, this is unimportant. We may compare, with Stough, the example of Simmias' height.[12] The explanation of Simmias' being smaller than Phaedo that Plato rejects is 'because he is Simmias'. Stough remarks that if this were the explanation of Simmias' being smaller than Phaedo, it would also explain his being taller than Socrates. This example would, I think, illustrate the second sort of contradiction that interests Plato just as well as the case of A and B that he in fact offers us. The only advantage of taking A's being bigger than B and B's being smaller than A as his example here is that the head by which they differ in height is clearly one and the same head.)

The extent of our sympathy with Plato is now revealed. We too, no doubt, would be troubled if we thought that there were two different, and incompatible, explanations of one and the same state of affairs. We would, for instance, be troubled if we thought that $1+1=2$, and also $1/1=2$. But unlike Plato, we do not think that there *are* any cases like this. We would also no doubt be troubled if we thought that A had become bigger than B by eating a lot, and B had become smaller than A by eating a lot. But we do not think that there are any cases of this kind either. It is not, then, that Plato has unusual assumptions about the nature of explanation as such (we will examine these in detail shortly); but rather, that when he considers explanation, he displays his customary misunderstanding of the relation of context to contradiction.

One final point is worth making here. It is sometimes suggested that the theory of Forms is simply a theory about universals.[13] We will examine the relation between Forms and universals in due course. But it is worth noting here that the explanations Plato rejects of the coming into being of two – addition and division – would be thought by many philosophers to be the universals that explain, or stand over, the many different particular instances of addition and division. As such, they would indeed both explain some cases of the coming into being of two. But Plato's misunderstanding of context and contradiction prompts him to look beyond universals here, when seeking non-contradictory explanations, and turn to Forms.

The Third Case of Contradiction

We have so far examined two cases of contradiction presented by our customary explanations. But there is also a third case of contradiction that Plato mentions in this passage that is very different from the two cases we have examined so far. And it is worth going into this third case of contradiction here because, as we shall see, it is Plato's desire to avoid contradiction of this sort that leads him to set up the most contentious element in his theory of explanation.

So far, the contradictions we have studied have lain between three items – two explanations of one state of affairs (in the first case), or one explanation of two opposed states of affairs (in the second case). In this third case, however, the contradiction lies in one explanation of one state of affairs – A's being bigger than B by a head (B's being smaller than A is not in question here, though it was involved earlier).

The contradiction is supposed to be made manifest if we reconstrue 'A is bigger than B by a head' as 'A is bigger than B by a small thing' (101a6-10: there can be no doubt that Plato does suppose this to be a further case of self-contradiction – the *teras* of 101b1 is clearly part of the *enantios logos* of 101a5-6). It may be helpful to compare and contrast here what Plato thinks is the true explanation in this case: 'A is bigger than B by the Form Big'. We may perhaps reformulate this as 'A is bigger than B by a big thing' (see pp.77-8 below).

It is still not clear, however, why Plato thinks that the first of these explanations is self-contradictory, but the second is not. But it may be possible to make further progress here, if we reformulate these explanations once more. We find that some of the explanations discussed later in this passage readily assume a propositional form.[14] In particular, if we look to 102bc once more, we find that Simmias is big not because he is Simmias, but because he participates in the Form Big. Here, then, both the accepted and the rejected explanation assume a propositional form. Now A's size is (really) to be explained in just the same way as Simmias'. So we can reformulate the explanation of this as 'A is big because he participates in the Form Big, which is a big thing'. The supposedly self-contradictory explanation, if rendered into parallel form, would read 'A is big, because he participates in (?=has) a head, which is a small thing'. This is at last beginning to look self-contradictory. It certainly would be contradictory to explain A's being taller than B by reference to something short about A (by reference to his short legs, for instance). At the same time, the last reformulation of this supposedly contradictory explanation is unsound. For A is not, after all, supposed to be taller than B because he has a head (whatever the size of the head), but because he has a head *more* than B. And Plato does seem to be aware of this in *Hippias Major* 294b, where the bigger is bigger *toi hyperechein* 'by exceeding'. And if once the explanation 'by a head' is seen to be short for 'by exceeding by a head', then it becomes much harder to see it as self-contradictory. None the less, Plato clearly *does* regard it as self-contradictory; and the only possible explanation of this seems to me to be the one I have suggested, unsound though it is.

An Argument for the Theory of Forms?

We have now examined in some detail the problems Plato sets out in *Phaedo* 96ff. When we come to consider the solutions he offers of these problems in *Phaedo* 101-2, we will find that the theory of Forms plays a crucial role here for Plato. *Prima facie*, then, Plato would seem to be saying 'Here is a problem that calls for us to posit the existence of Forms'; and so it would seem that his argument in this passage gives us a reason for believing in the theory of Forms that is independent of the arguments Plato offers for the theory elsewhere.

But this picture is complicated by Socrates' introduction here of the hypothetical method. The resolution of Socrates' problems about explanation in fact serves as an illustration of this method. Socrates is said, at 100b5-7, to *hypothesize* the existence of Forms – ὑποθέμενος εἶναί τι καλὸν αὐτὸ καθ᾽ αὑτὸ καὶ ἀγαθὸν καὶ μέγα καὶ τἆλλα πάντα. So it might seem that Plato is not presenting us here with an argument for the existence of Forms after all. For we are told initially to hypothesize their existence, and subsequently, that the initial hypotheses, εἰ πισταὶ ὑμῖν εἰσιν, ὅμως ἐπισκεπτέαι σαφέστερον (107b5-6). Certainly, Socrates does say that he hypothesizes ἑκάστοτε λόγον ὃν ἂν κρίνω ἐρρωμενέστατον (100a4); but he does not tell us how to judge which hypothesis *is* the best here, nor does he tell us how to judge the best of those hypotheses that are above it, when he introduces this concept in 101d7.

There must be some doubt, then, as to whether Plato thought that *Phaedo* 96-102 constituted an argument for the theory of Forms. But we should ask, not just whether Plato regarded this passage as an argument for the theory of Forms, but whether we ourselves should so regard it. And the answer to this latter question, I think, is clearly 'yes'. For the hypothesis that there are Forms is not an unargued assumption, but rather, as we shall see, is the natural conclusion of Plato's line of thought. It is clear, I think, that Plato's problems with explanation would have given him a reason for believing in the existence of Forms, even had he had no other reason for doing so.

Forms and Explanation

We have seen that two of the three cases of self-contradiction Plato finds in our customary explanations arise from the same misunderstanding of the relation of context to contradiction, on his part, that we have already witnessed in chapters 2 and 3. It should come as no surprise, then, to find that the theory of Forms once again plays a crucial role in the resolution of the problem here.

Forms are posited here as explanations that do not suffer from any of the three forms of self-contradiction we have examined. The resolution of our problems is thus very easy. Socrates' first example concerns the Form Beautiful; this is said to explain *all* cases of beauty (100d7-8 cf 100c4-5, where it explains all cases of beauty except itself). So, when we turn back to the case of the coming into being of two, we find that there are not, on Socrates' hypothesis, two competing and incompatible explanations of different cases of the same phenomenon, but just one explanation – participation in the Form Two – which explains all such cases. And when we turn to the second form of contradiction, we find that there too, the hypothesis that there are Forms, and that Forms function as explanations, resolves the difficulties. We learn from 100e5-6 that it is the Form Big that renders big things big, and bigger things bigger; and that the Form Small similarly renders small things small, and smaller things smaller. So, in our example of the two men who differ in height by a head, Socrates now instructs us to say that A is now bigger than B by the Form Big, and B is smaller than B by the Form Small. This means that we now have one explanation of A's smallness, and another, opposed, explanation of the opposed phenomenon, B's bigness. So here too, the hypothesis that there are Forms that function as explanations resolves Plato's difficulty. Finally, if we suppose that the Form Big is a big thing (or at least not a small thing), and if the Form Small is a small thing (or at least not a big thing), Forms as explanations will also escape the third form of contradiction. (We will return later to the question, whether we should make this supposition).

But Forms are not the only kind of uncontradictory explanation. Plato's 'subtle' reasons, introduced later (104b), also avoid the three forms of contradiction. These are, in fact, unlike Forms as explanations, very much what the unphilosophical man would give as explanations; and yet, unlike the non-philosopher's explanation of height, they prove acceptable to Socrates.

The reason why these unphilosophical explanations meet the requirements on explanation seems to be that in these cases, the non-philosopher's explanation could be explained in turn by a Socratic 'simple' explanation. For it becomes clear from 105bc, that a safe, simple, answer is also possible in all those cases where a subtle explanation can be given. Socrates' point in this passage is just that, even though both sorts of answer are possible, he is now interested in discussing the subtle kind. Presumably if an objector challenged a subtle explanation – if, for instance, we told him that something was hot because of fire (i.e. perhaps because it was fire, or perhaps because it was on fire), and he then asked 'But why is fire hot?', we would reply 'by participating in the Form Hot', thus returning to the safe and simple answer. Thus for Plato, Forms are epistemologically prior to clever explanations; and the explanatory relation is transitive: if P explains Q, and Q explains R, then P explains R too.

In 104d11ff. Socrates lays out the conditions for being a 'subtle' explanation. A subtle explanation always participates in a given Form, which is one of a pair of opposites. Not only can the subtle explanation not bear the attribute of the Form opposed to the Form in which it always participates, it also cannot bear any attribute that implies this opposed Form. Subtle explanations thus resemble Forms, and the smallness in Simmias, which both never partake in what is opposed to them, rather than Simmias himself, who can participate in the opposed Forms in question simultaneously – and presumably does so, throughout the course of his existence (cf 102bd). And it is this close relationship of 'subtle' explanations to Forms that enables them too to function as uncontradictory explanations.

Plato, Russell, and the Third Man Regress

The third man regress argument against the theory of Forms is now generally agreed to rest on three principles, labelled in most discussions One Over Many (OM), Nonidentity (NI) and Self-predication (SP) – though there is still no agreement as to exactly how these principles should be formulated. I shall argue that in fact we find here not just a One Over Many argument for the theory of Forms, but also that Plato shows some interest here in combining all three principles on which the regress depends in a theory of explanation; and further, that Plato might reasonably (though wrongly as it turns out) have supposed that a theory of explanation could rest on these three principles.

The three principles, I believe, form the background of assumptions against which the argument is conducted. We can see this most clearly, I believe, if we compare Plato's practice in the *Phaedo* with that of Russell in his *The Problems of Philosophy*. For there, Russell undertakes to uphold an updated version of the theory of Forms, in the chapter 'The World of Universals'; and in the course of his argument, he discussed all three principles that figure in the third man regress.

Russell's first task there is to establish that there are such things as universals. To this end, he writes 'If we ask ourselves what justice is, it is natural to proceed by considering this, that, and the other just act, with a view to discovering what they have in common. They must all, in some sense, partake of a common nature, which will be found in whatever is just and in nothing else. This common nature, in virtue of which they are all just, will be justice itself...' (p.52). 'Justice itself', a Russellian universal, is thus derived from an application of OM. Now this principle plays a major role in Plato's, as in Russell's view of explanation. For, as Fine has noted, an OM principle of some sort is clearly enunciated in *Phaedo* 100d7-8: τῷ καλῷ πάντα τὰ καλὰ καλά. It may, perhaps, be the case that Plato would apply this principle only over a small range of cases;[16] that this is an OM principle, and that it lies at the heart of the view that there are Forms that are explanations seems to be beyond dispute.

And when we turn to the second of the three principles on which the third man regress depends, NI, we once again find in Russell a clear statement, both of the principle itself, and of its role in his theory of explanation. He writes 'the idea justice is not identical with anything that is just: it is something other than particular things, which particular things partake of. Not being a particular, it cannot exist in the world of sense' (p.52). Now Plato simply takes it for granted in the *Phaedo* that Forms do not exist in the world of sense. But there is a good reason why he should believe this which is made explicit at *Hippias Major* 297a2-3. There, Socrates says to Hippias, 'But the explanation, Hippias, is non-identical with what it is the explanation of'.

Russell's theory of explanation is at this point complete. He places no reliance, himself, on the third of the three principles on which the third man regress rests, SP.[17] And this is just as well, as it means that his theory of explanation is certainly not liable to the third man regress. But it does, at least as I have hitherto set it up, suffer from a shortcoming of which Plato's theory of explanation is often accused – namely, that it is not explanatory. Russell tells us *that* what particular just acts have in common is participation in some sense in the universal, justice. And he thus suggests that there exists something apart from particular just acts, the universal, justice; but he has not thereby *explained* particular just acts, in the sense that he has not told us *why* we call just these acts just acts, or, in other words, how we group together this particular Many, under this One.

Now it is, as I have said, common for Plato to be criticized on similar grounds: and commentators sometimes reply to such criticism that Plato is not telling us the whole story in this passage, and that we must understand Forms here as definitions, if we are to find a general theory of explanation in this passage.[18] Now that is certainly one way of supplementing OM and NI to give a general theory of explanation; but it is not the only possible such supplement. We have seen that in Plato's subsequent criticism of the theory of Forms, he employs not just OM and NI, but also a third principle, SP. And this principle too, might be used to supplement OM and NI to produce a theory of truly explanatory explanations.

To see how this would work, let us return once more to Russell's theory of explanation. As I have said, Russell's theory does not involve SP; and Russell simply does not tackle the question of *how* to group a Many under a One. But he does, curiously enough, catch the force of SP in this regard, when he considers an objection to his own theory of explanation. When Russell considers the view that there are no universals, but only particulars, he makes the following remark about triangle and white: 'If we wish to avoid the universals whiteness and triangularity, we shall choose some particular patch of white or some particular triangle and say that anything is white or a triangle, if it has the right sort of resemblance to our chosen particular' (p.55). Resemblance to a paradigm instance of white or triangle, here, serves to group together particular whites or particular triangles.

Now Russell does *not* here express SP, as it is thought of in connection with the theory of Forms. SP there consists in the view that the One (that is, the Form) has the characteristic that is shared by the Many (that is, the particulars) over which it stands; whereas Russell here is envisaging that there is not a One that stands over the Many, but that the Many all resemble (or are identical with) one of themselves. But the basic explanatory idea would be the same: that the many particular whites, triangles, and so on, are grouped together by the right sort of resemblance to something white, triangular, and so on. It seems perfectly possible, then, that Plato might supplement OM and NI with SP to form a theory of explanation.[19]

If we are to attribute a general theory of explanation to Plato, then, it seems we must attribute to him either a theory of self-predicative universals, or a theory of definitions. Given that these seem to be the possible options, we must look to the text to decide which of them we find (if, indeed, we find either). Unfortunately, there is no clear and unambiguous evidence in either direction. And it may be, that Plato would, if challenged to explain how we are to group a Many under a One, call in the definitions of the individual Forms at this point. But it may also be that Plato did at this time believe in a theory of paradigmatic universals. Plato leaves the nature of the participation relation very vague in 100d5-6, where he speaks of participation 'by presence, communion, or whatever the manner and nature of the relation may be' (Gallop). But there is at least one pointer in the direction of self-predicative Forms that we have witnessed. And that is Plato's belief that it is contradictory for A's being big to be explained by a small thing. This does suggest that Plato did think that resemblance was involved in the explanatory relation, and that he at least had some interest here in a theory of self-predicative Forms.

Plato does here, then, show some interest in all three principles on which the third man regress is subsequently built; and not only are all three principles available to Plato, he also seems interested in setting up a series of explanations akin to the later regress. We have seen that for Plato, the explanatory relation is transitive: an initial *explanandum* is explained by a 'clever' explanation, which is in turn explained by a Form. But the Form is still an explanation of the original *explanandum*. In the third man regress, only the *dramatis personae* have changed, as the explanatory relation runs from particular to Form to second Form. The regress, then, may be a real objection to Plato's theory of Forms, and depend on principles which underlie the argument we find in *Phaedo* 96ff. for the hypothesis that there are Forms.

Conclusion

In this chapter, I have argued that Aristotle was right in identifying a One Over Many argument as an important argument for the theory of Forms. I have contended that this argument is concerned with Plato's view of explanation, against a background of presuppositions that have led other philosophers to a theory of universals. Plato's argument, however, leads him to a theory of Forms instead. I have suggested that this may occur because of his misunderstanding of the relation of context to contradiction.

In chapter 5, I shall draw together various strands in chapters 2-4, and argue that my account of the different arguments for Forms enables us to give a coherent account of why Forms have the properties they do. I shall present an analysis of what is perhaps their most important, and certainly their most puzzling characteristic, in terms of Plato's interest in contradiction.

NOTES

1. See Fine 'One over Many' 213 n.25.

2. 'Forms and First Principles' 277-9.

3. 'One over Many' 214.

4. 'Reasons and Causes' 87-8.

5. See too 'Reasons and Causes' 99 n.61.

6. Crombie takes a similar view of some of the puzzles (161). He also finds in Socrates' retreat to *logoi* some evidence that he is interested in the *a priori* (167).

7. This objection, that the clever explanations are diverse in character, tells against any form of the view that our ordinary explanations are potentially contradictory because they are of the wrong sort. Such views are advanced by e.g. Burge, 'The Idea as *Aitiai* in the *Phaedo*' who believes that explanations should be analytic (8) and by Gallop, who believes that they should be constitutive (174, 185 and 187).

8. *Plato* 169.

9. The following account of 'causal field' is drawn from pp.21-3. See also his *The Cement of the Universe* 35. The notion is first set out by Anderson 'The Problem of Causality' 132-3.

10. 'Causes and Conditions' 23. A similar example, this time concerning a singular causal statement, is given by van Fraasen, in 'The Pragmatics Of Explanation'. He refers (144) to the 'classic case' of the *paresis* example. In this example, the question 'why did the mayor contract paresis?' may mean 'why did the mayor, in contrast to other townfolk generally, contract paresis?'; or it may mean, 'why did he contract it, in contrast to the other syphilitics in the country club?' (147). He speaks here of 'context-dependency' and 'determining contextual factors' (48).

11. Vlastos discusses Plato's concern with contradiction in 'Reasons and Causes' n.57 and 100-1 n.64. He gives substantially the right account of this, but he completely fails to see its significance. Similarly, Gosling also sees the right answer, only to reject it. 'It might well strike us that when Plato complains that the explanation equally well explains opposite circumstances, he is making an elementary mistake. Yet this is very likely Plato's point...' (*Plato* 169).

12. 'Forms and Explanations in the *Phaedo*' 18.

13. Thus G. E. Moore writes in *Some Main Problems of Philosophy* that 'Plato's theory of ideas is in fact just a theory about universals' (353).

14. C. C. W. Taylor has suggested that the clever explanation 'by snow', may naturally be expanded as 'because it *is* snow' ('Forms as Causes in the *Phaedo*' 49). Stough, however, suggests that one of Plato's problems is that he does *not* formulate his explanations as propositions (10). So too Burge 4-5.

15. Cf. Crombie 158. This rules out the view of F. C. White, 'The *Phaedo* and *Republic* V on Essences'. White believes that when we ask why x is F, we need only appeal to something other than F itself in those cases where x is contingently, and not necessarily, F. White's view of the argument as a whole suffers because he does not see its relation to the principle OM, and to the theory of explanation more generally (see in particular pp.154-5 of his article).

16. It is important to remember that in this passage, Plato's main concern is to contrast Forms as explanations with the rejected everyday explanations. It is nonetheless clear at 100d7ff. that, just as the one Form Beautiful explains all the many particular beautiful things, so too the one Form Big explains all the particular big and bigger things. But perhaps the principle should not be extended to cover cases where there is no problem with our everyday explanations.

17. Russell in fact generates a wide range of universals by OM: 'nearly all the words to be found in the dictionary stand for universals' (53); all verbs do so (53), and so do relations expressed by propositions' (53-4). In 'Edinburgh is to the north of London', 'to the north of' is a universal (56). There is clearly no

room for SP in this theory of Russell's then. And this enables us to see also what a wide range of Forms is generated by the unrestricted application of OM.

18. Vlastos, 'Reasons and Causes' 91-2 n.44 and Crombie ii 162, take this view, among many others.

19. I here follow Strang, 'Plato and the Third Man'. Strang formulates the explanatory model as follows (196): 'A thing is an X, if and only if it resembles the Form X'. He takes the surely correct view that 'the OM is, if anything, a logical reason for generating Forms ... Plato's motive for postulating paradigmatic Forms was epistemological' (194-5).

5. PLATO'S CONCEPTION OF FORMS

Introduction

I suggested in chapter 1, that if we were to give a satisfactory answer to the question 'why did Plato have a theory of Forms?', we had to explain firstly why Plato departed from the ontology of the Socratic dialogues; secondly why he posited the existence of Forms, rather than something different; and thirdly why Plato took this course, when other philosophers have not done so.

We have now made some progress towards answering this last question by attributing to Plato a misunderstanding of the relation of context to contradiction; and we have seen how this misunderstanding led Plato to depart from Socratic ontology, when it was coupled with some perfectly natural views about knowledge and explanation. We have also seen in general terms how Forms differ from particulars: that Forms, unlike particulars, are adequate as objects of knowledge and as explanations; and that Forms, like the logical parts of particulars, but unlike particulars themselves, do not admit of the sort of apparent contradiction we examined in chapter 2. But we have not as yet seen what the relation is between these very general differences between Forms and particulars, and the more specific set of attributes that Plato ascribes to Forms – that they exist forever, are pure, unmixed, unchanging, 'in every way being', 'in themselves', and stand in relation to particulars as a model does to copies of it.

In this chapter, then, I propose to ask why Plato does ascribe these specific properties to Forms; and to argue that Plato's goal here is to safeguard Forms from real or apparent contradiction. A complete immunity from all contradiction is very much what we would expect to characterize Forms given the account I have offered of Plato's arguments for the theory of Forms. We should note in passing that to the extent that this is so, the theory of Forms does display some coherency (cf. Cross and Woozley, quoted on p.16 above, and Annas, quoted on p.48 above) – a coherency arising from Plato's view of the relation between context and contradiction.

It is often not hard to see why Plato ascribes specific properties to Forms. Forms are said to be pure and unmixed (*eilikrines, Phaedo* 66a3, *monoeides, Phaedo* 78d5, *katharon, Phaedo* 79d2), because they do not suffer from the form of apparent self-contradiction we examined in chapter 2; for the same reason, Forms are not composed of logical parts, but are each 'one' (*Republic* 476a5, 507b). Forms are unchanging (*Phaedo* 78d4-7) and exist forever, because they could not otherwise be a source of knowledge, as we saw in chapter 3. And we have also seen in those chapters, why Plato should stress that Forms are *kath' hauta*, 'in themselves'.

But there are two properties Plato ascribes to Forms that do not, at first, seem to fit so well with this line of thought – that they are 'separate' from particulars, and that they are paradigms, in some sense. And the remarks made by the young Socrates in the *Parmenides* that he has a problem in deciding just what things there are forms of, also merit discussion.

Let us turn first to this question.

The Range of the Theory of Forms

Socrates says in *Parmenides* 130, that he is sure that there are Forms of Just, Beautiful, Good and so on; that he is in *aporia* as to whether there are Forms of Man, Fire and Water; and he is shown first denying that there are Forms of laughable things like hair and mud, but then immediately wondering whether there may not be such Forms after all.

Now Socrates does not really tell us why he has these difficulties in deciding what there are Forms of. He merely says, about the last group, (1) that these things are as we see them to be, and (2) that he is afraid it may be too ridiculous to hold that there are Forms of such things. (2) need not detain us. Parmenides answers this point by telling Socrates that he is still young, and has not yet become fully involved in philosophy. The implication – that, if this is all that worries him, Socrates should summon up his courage and admit Forms of Mud, Dirt and Hair – is clear.

But Socrates is still in doubt here, though, whether there are Forms of things that are as we see them to be – and perhaps this category covers Man, Fire, and Water, as well as Hair, Mud and Dirt. And this is puzzling, in so far as the arguments for the existence of Forms that we have examined in chapters 3 and 4 are arguments for the existence of Forms for all predicates. In chapter 3, I suggested that men die, fires are extinguished, and water evaporates – and so there can be no knowledge of sensible men, fires or water, which should lead us to posit Forms of these entities. And in chapter 4, I suggested that the OM assumption is in play – and this too leads us to posit Forms for all predicates.

Nonetheless it is, I believe, explicable that Socrates should here express doubts about the range of the theory of Forms. We should bear in mind, firstly, that the theory of Forms is under attack in the *Parmenides*, and secondly, that Socrates has just, at this point in the dialogue, formulated the line of thought we find in *Republic* VII as a formal argument for the theory of Forms (see chapter 2, pp.43-45 above). I suggested in chapter 2, that this argument does, in fact, lead us just to posit Forms of things that are not as we see them to be – and so it is not, perhaps, surprising that Socrates should here express more certainty that there are Forms of such things (Like, Unlike, Beautiful and so on) than that there are Forms of things that are as we see them to be. Nor is it surprising that Socrates should revert to the ideas of *Republic* VII when the theory of Forms is under attack. For we saw in chapter 2, that the new philosopher's route to the theory of Forms departs from reflection on things that are not as they seem (such as the size of the middle finger). And if this is not certain, then the whole theory of Forms is not certain.

All in all, then, it is not entirely surprising that Socrates should say here that he is sure that there are Forms of some things, but unsure whether there are Forms of everything.

Let us now turn to the question of the 'separation' of Forms.

Forms and Separation

Vlastos speaks of the 'participation' of particulars in Forms as designating a 'one-way relation of ontological dependence between temporal things and eternal Forms' ('Reasons and Causes', p.86). The idea is, that a Form Chiliagon can exist without instantiation by particular chiliagons, but particular chiliagons could not exist unless there were a Form Chiliagon in which they participated. It is, of course, a consequence of this view that Forms are entirely separate from particulars.

Now Rohr has argued convincingly, in his 'Plato on Empty Forms', that Vlastos has rather overstated the case here. He shows that all Forms are instantiated at some time or other. Nonetheless, Rohr does accept that there may be a temporary lack of particular instances of a given Form; and that the creation in the *Timaeus* suggests that 'all or most Forms exist before their instances' (see p.279). It is hard to dispute, then, that Forms do not exist 'in' particulars, nor that the continued existence of a Form is dependent on its continued instantiation by particulars.

We must ask, then, whether these doctrines (I shall refer to them as the separation of Forms and the ontological independence of Forms) can be explained on the account I have offered of Plato's arguments for the theory of Forms.

Now Plato may well have more than one reason for holding that Forms are separate from particulars, and ontologically independent of them. One reason may be Plato's views about recollection, and the immortality of the soul. If (as Plato claims) we know Forms before birth, and before we first encounter sensible particulars, this might be one reason for supposing that Forms are separate from particulars, and ontologically independent of them.

But I believe that Plato also had another reason for holding this view about Forms – and one which derives, indirectly, from the arguments for the theory of Forms that we have examined in chapters 2-4. We have seen there that Forms are non-identical with particulars. Thus they must either exist separately from particulars, or exist 'in' them (as 'logical' parts, or as an Aristotelian universal might). Now we know that Forms must always exist, and must always remain the same. But particulars, as we know, are in a process of constant gradual change throughout their existence, and that sooner or later they all perish.[1] We must ask then what the fate is of the logical parts (or alternatively the universals) that are in them. Well, Plato does not discuss the possibility that there are universals in particulars; but he does tell us, in *Phaedo* 102-3, that when particulars undergo change, or perish, their logical parts either retreat or themselves perish. (The examples he discusses make it clear that he thinks that some retreat while others perish.) But Forms obviously cannot perish on such occasions; and so it seems that they cannot exist in particulars. They will be like the logical parts of particulars in many ways, of course; but they will be unlike them in being separate from particulars, and ontologically independent of them.

So let us now turn to the question of Forms and paradigmatism, and ask whether here too, Plato has reasons connected with his view of contradiction, for thinking of Forms as paradigms.

Forms, Paradigmatism, and Self-predication

In chapter 4, we saw that it may be an essential feature of the theory of explanation Plato advances in the *Phaedo*, that Forms serve as paradigms. We were compelled to admit, though, that this aspect of the theory of explanation there is not a consequence of Plato's view of the relation of context to contradiction. The question we face, then, is whether this property of Forms is compatible with the other properties Forms enjoy as objects of knowledge, and as pure, unmixed beings, or whether Plato's theory is incoherent at this point.

I shall argue that the properties Forms possess that indicate their paradigmatic function are indeed compatible with their other properties; and further, that these properties may in fact, despite appearances, be derived from the Forms' lack of self-contradiction. I shall suggest that it is one of Plato's central contentions, that for any predicate F, the Form F, unlike particular F's, holds the predicate F essentially, rather than accidentally; and that for this reason, it will not admit of any predicate opposed to this predicate F.

To claim that Forms hold some predicates essentially, is to present a picture of a much more subtle Plato than is currently fashionable. For it is generally thought that while Plato is able to distinguish identity from predication in the later dialogues, he is confused about such matters in his middle period. Thus C. C. W. Taylor thinks that in *Protagoras* 330-331, Plato is confused between being an attribute and having it; Gallop suggests that in *Phaedo* 74bc, Plato is confused between the predicative function of the verb 'to be', and its role as an identity sign; and Owen has diagnosed some of the puzzles in the second part of the *Parmenides* as resting on what he calls I/P confusion, but sees in the *Sophist* a final, successful, attempt to clear up this error.[2] But just as Parmenides was once thought to be confused between the existential and the copulative uses of *einai* (by Kirk and Raven, for instance), but is now thought to exploit links between these two uses of the verb (by Owen), or to employ a 'fused' concept of being (by Furth), so too Plato, I believe, is a good deal more subtle than commentators have made out.[3] We will find that Plato is not confused between identity and predication but exploits a link between identity and predication, with the notion of essential predication.

Commentators who hold that Plato is confused, rely on texts such as those mentioned above, which, they believe, display the confusion when we analyze them. So obviously, I must, in due course, give a satisfactory analysis of these texts that does not attribute to Plato a confusion between identity and predication. But as it is also sometimes remarked that both identity and predication typically have the form 'S is P', and that this may have been what led Plato to confuse the two,[4] I shall first try to show that even in his middle period, Plato had unambiguous paraphrases of the ambiguous form 'S is P' at his disposal. This will enable us to conclude that if Plato ever was confused about the logical status of a proposition of the form 'S is P', then he was wilfully confused – that he could have distinguished between the two possible readings of such a proposition, if he had so desired.

I shall argue that some passages in Plato (including some uncontroversial ones, I hope) present us with arguments that depend on our making a threefold distinction, between (a) identity, (b) essential predication, and (c) accidental predication; and that these passages provide us with linguistic evidence that Plato could make such a distinction. I shall then turn to the disputed passages from the *Protagoras* and the *Phaedo*, which do not provide us with linguistic evidence that Plato has this threefold distinction in mind there. I shall argue that none the less, these passages can be interpreted most plausibly in the light of this threefold distinction that we find when Plato discusses similar subjects in other contexts.

Let us turn first then, to *Phaedo* 102-3, a passage in which both Plato's argument, and his linguistic usage, provide evidence that we must make a threefold distinction. Most commentators in fact agree that we find such a threefold distinction in this passage. Sometimes commentators appeal to the linguistic contrast between πεφυκέναι on the one hand, and τῷ μεγέθει ὃ τυγχάνει ἔχων on the other hand, in 102c1-2, as evidence that Plato had the contrast between essential and accidental predication in mind here.[5] This linguistic contrast, however, does not subsequently recur in the argument, as Hackforth has pointed out.[6] But O'Brien has also pointed to Plato's use of *anangke* in 104d2 and 104d6 to indicate an essential predication ('odd' is an essential predicate of 'three'); and (in a footnote) to Plato's use of the temporal qualification *aei* to make essential predications in the argument.[7] And it is Plato's use of temporal qualifications that seems to me to be significant indication that he has indeed made the threefold distinction between identity, essential predication, and accidental predication.

In the final argument for immortality, Plato is concerned with change through time. The argument turns on the fact that there are no dead souls: 'dead soul' is a contradiction in terms, just like 'hot snow'. Souls, Socrates argues, are essentially alive, just as snow is essentially cold.

The case of Socrates and the predicate 'small' is taken to exemplify accidental predication, whereas fire and snow, with the predicates 'hot' and 'cold' exemplify essential predication. The point is clearly made that Socrates retains his identity when the accidental predicate 'short' becomes true of him. The Greek is ἔτι ὢν ὅσπερ εἰμί, οὗτος ὁ αὐτὸς σμικρός εἰμι (102e4-5). But fire, for instance, is no longer fire if it is not hot, or if it becomes cold. The Greek, once again, is ἔτι εἶναι ὅπερ ἦν (103d7, 103d12). (The parallel is deliberate as 103d12 makes clear.)

These cases of identity, then, seem to be quite straightforward. Socrates' identity as Socrates, and fire's identity as fire, would be hard to get confused about. And when Socrates says that he is the same man οὗτος ὁ αὐτός, it is obvious that Plato is using the phrase ἔτι εἶναι ὅπερ ἦν as a formula to express identity.

Let us now consider accidental predication. Once again, we would not anticipate that this could cause Plato any difficulty. It would be hard to mistake an accidental predication such as 'Socrates is small', for an identity. And the sense of the passage shows that Plato does not make this error. If he thought that Socrates was identical with small or big, he would not hold that Socrates can change between the two without losing his identity. This is also reflected in the Greek: the accidental predication is expressed by the phrase 'having smallness' (102c3).

What, then, of the essential predication? Does Plato mistake essential predications such as 'fire is hot' for identities? The answer is surely 'no'. Socrates first asks for an ontological commitment from Cebes with the question θερμόν τι καλεῖς καὶ ψυχρόν; (103c11).[8] Next, Socrates clearly establishes the nonidentity of fire with hot and of snow with cold: ἕτερόν τι πυρὸς τὸ θερμὸν καὶ ἕτερόν τι χιόνος τὸ ψυχρόν; (103d2-3). Here, *heteron* marks the notion of identity, just as *ho autos* does in 102e4-4, and the phrase ... (οὐκ) εἶναι ὅπερ ἦν ... is once again employed (103d7). The predicates are, once again, something that fire and snow 'have'. But they are distinguished from accidental predicates by the temporal qualification on 'having' – ὅτανπερ ᾖ, 'throughout their existence' (103e5).

We have now seen, then, that Plato did have the linguistic resources to disambiguate propositions of the form 'S is P'. He had only to ask himself whether the proposition in question would be paraphrased with *tauton* on the one hand, or as S's 'having' P on the other. But this is not, as yet, to claim that there are no ambiguous propositions of the form 'S is P' in Plato. For it remains perfectly possible that Plato simply did not ask himself the relevant question on some occasions.[9] Moreover, we have not as yet examined any proposition of the form 'the S is S'. And propositions of this form are thought to post an additional problem for Plato in so far as the same word 'S' stands on both sides of the verb.[10]

Now there is in fact an example of a proposition of this form in the text we have been discussing, *Phaedo* 102-3. In 102e5-6, it is said of the big in us that it οὐ τετόλμηκεν μέγα ὂν σμικρὸν εἶναι. Here, at least, we find 'big' and 'small' on either side of the verb *einai*. We must ask then, whether Plato clearly regards this as a predication, whether he clearly regards it as an identity, or whether he confuses these two alternatives. I shall argue that the proposition expresses an essential predication.

The big in us and the small in us are clearly subsumed under a general rule given in 102e7-103a2: no opposite can ἔτι εἶναι ὅπερ ἦν and at the same time τοὐναντίον γίγνεσθαί τε καὶ εἶναι. Now we have seen that ἔτι εἶναι ὅπερ ἦν is a formula used by Plato to express identity. But we have not met τοὐναντίον γίγνεσθαί τε καὶ εἶναι before. It is not immediately clear, then, whether Plato's point is that opposites cannot both retain their identity, and also lose their identity ('becoming and being the opposite'), or whether his point is that opposites cannot both retain their identity and 'become and be the opposite' in the sense of bearing an opposed predicate.

The meaning of the phrase 'become and be the opposite' can, however, be clarified. For Plato goes on to refer to the process in question by the words τούτῳ τῷ παθήματι (103a1-2). And in Plato, as in Aristotle, a thing's *pathe* are its predicates. (A nearby example occurs in 104a4, where it is said that three *peponthe* odd.) What Socrates is telling us here, then, is that the big in us could not become small (i.e. admit 'small' as a predicate) and still 'be what it was' (i.e. retain its identity). Or, in other words, that 'big' is an essential predicate of the big in us.[11]

And we can extend the moral to cover the Forms themselves. For the Form Big equally will not be both big and small, but just big (102d6-e2). And it is plainly thought to be on a par with the big in us in this respect.

Thus we see that the case of the predicate 'big', and the big in us parallels that of the predicate 'hot', and fire. 'Fire is fire' and 'the big in us is the big is us' are identities. 'Fire is hot', on the other hand, and 'the big in us is big', are essential predications. We can see now the link between identity and essential predication that I spoke of earlier (see p.87 above). If we say that 'x is not hot', we are giving information both about its predicates, and also about its identity. That is to say, we know (a) that 'hot' is a not one of its predicates, and (b) that it is not identical with fire.

Now the difference between the accidental and the essential predication is linguistically marked in this passage by the temporal qualifications Plato employs: 'always' (e.g. 104a6), 'never' (e.g. 102d7), and 'throughout its existence' (e.g. 103e5). It is natural that temporal language should be to the fore in a passage where temporal change is under discussion. And one aspect of the contrast between Forms and particulars is that Forms are always the same, whereas particulars change. But this is not all there is to the contrast between essential and accidental predication, or to the contrast between Forms and particulars. Nor, indeed, is it the only way to present the temporal aspect of this contrast.

In chapter 3, I have argued that the argument from flux turns on the fact that particulars have different (and incompatible) attributes at different times, and that different tokens of the same type may equally enjoy different (and incompatible) attributes. And I also argued there that Plato is, in *Republic* V, concerned to view Forms and particulars from a timeless standpoint. If this is right, and if Plato is concerned to contrast particulars with Forms there, then we must expect that he will employ some form of qualification to indicate that Forms hold their predicates essentially, whereas particulars do not, but that this qualification will not be a temporal qualification. And this, of course, is precisely what we find. There are, as we saw in chapter 3, two extremes of being, the *pantelos on* and the *medamei on* (see 477a). Between these two poles are located the intermediate things that partake of both being and notbeing (478e1-2).

It is worth dwelling awhile on this nontemporal form of qualification that Plato applies to predications here. A consideration of some further examples will confirm that qualifications of this form are analogous to the temporal qualifications of the *Phaedo*. Moreover, it may render my claims about *Phaedo* 74 and *Protagoras* 331 more convincing, to show that elsewhere Plato can be cleared of I/P confusion, if we make a distinction between accidental and essential predication.

I shall first consider two passages in the *Parmenides*, 137c, and 146b-147a, which are among those thought by Owen to rest on I/P confusion. Only the second of these two passages employs what I might style the language of essential predication; but both, I believe, will yield a more interesting and plausible argument, if construed as resting on essential predication. And even in the *Parmenides*, I believe, we should prefer the most plausible interpretations of the arguments that we can find.

The ambiguous 'S is P' proposition on which the first bout of argument hangs is to be found in 137d3: εἰ ἕν ἔσται τὸ ἕν – 'if the One is one'.[12] The structure of the argument shows that this cannot be taken as a case of accidental predication; for if 'one' were an accidental predicate of the One, then 'many' might equally well be an accidental predicate of it. But throughout the first movement, 'many' is not considered to be a possible predicate of the One. Yet the Greek *metechein* (137e1,e6) and *echein* (138a1) show that predication, rather than identity, is involved. To say that Plato is suffering from I/P confusion is one possible response to these facts. But it is not the *only* possible response to them; for it is also possible to take 137c4-5, 137c9-d1 and 137d3 as expressing essential predications. In that case (if 'one' is thought of as an essential predicate of the One), there will be a perfectly good reason why the One cannot have 'many' as a predicate. If the One were (predicatively) not-one, it would no longer be the One, just as fire, if it were not hot, would no longer be fire.

There is not, in this argument, any Greek expression that marks off essential from accidental predication. But that omission is made good in a parallel argument that we find in *Sophist* 245a, about the Parmenidean One. When the question is raised there, whether the Parmenidean One is composed of parts, the discussion is carried on in terms of *pathe* (245a5, b4, c1-2) – predicates, that is. The argument is, that the Parmenidean One must be *ameres* ... *pantelos* (245a8), if it is to be one *pantelos* presumably. The Eleatic Visitor goes on to distinguish being one 'in some way' (*pos*), from being the One (245b8-9), which, if I am right, is 'in every way', or essentially, one. Robinson sets this down, in his *Plato's Earlier Dialectic*, as a passage in which Plato distinguishes identity from predication (p.252). On my view, Plato is also employing here a distinction between essential and accidental predication.

In the *Parmenides* itself, the *motif* of 'being in every way F' or 'in some way F', occurs very frequently (138d8, e6, 139c8, 140a3, b2, d5, 141e9-10, 157c, 159d, 163a), as we might expect in a work concerned with the compresence of opposites. Frede, who has noticed this fact, claims that in the *Parmenides*, from the fact that something is not x, it can be concluded that it is in no way x; and he diagnoses the error here as overlooking the distinction between two uses of '... is ...' (p.30). But a brief look at one of the arguments in the dialogue will, I believe, serve to dispel this idea.

In *Parmenides* 146-7, we find the qualifications *pei* (147a4) and *pantapasin* (147a6) on various predications. The One and the Notone are here taken to have 'one' and 'notone' respectively, as essential predicates. It is suggested here that 'one' is accidentally predicated of the notone. Plato makes it clear that the Notone would not thereby be rendered the One, but would just become 'one in some way'. But this is impossible – because the Notone is notone 'in every way', or essentially. If it were not 'notone in every way', it would not be the Notone. Owen writes of this: 'The negation is construed as denying that the subject is X both in identifying and in the predicative sense of the words' ('Notes on Ryle's Plato', pp.355-6). But this is just one more case in which a predication of the form '... is not x' legitimately carries implications as to the identity of the subject.

Now these texts are all more or less aporetic. It may, then, carry more conviction to point to one final instance of essential predication, from the second, positive, portion of the Sophist, before returning to the disputed texts of the middle period.

In the second part of the *Sophist*, Kinds commune, but not all Kinds commune with all other Kinds. This conclusion is established in 251d, when the notion of communion of Kinds is first introduced. Plato's refutation of the latelearners' position – that there is no communion of Kinds whatsoever – has attracted much attention of late. But modern commentators seem to share Theaetetus' view that the possibility that there is unlimited communion of Kinds, which is dismissed briefly in 252d, is both easy to refute, and philosophically uninteresting. In both arguments equally, however, we again meet the qualifications that betoken essential predication.

On the view that there is no communion, Motion and Rest in no way (*oudamei*) partake in Being (251e9); but on the view that there is unlimited communion, Motion and Rest would both in every way (*pantapasin* 251d6) be moving and at rest. Motion, however, is in every way (*pantapasin*, 255e11) different from Rest. This, I believe, is because what is in no way (*medamos*) at rest is in motion (251d1). Once we have put in the appropriate qualifications, either 'in motion' or 'at rest' applies exclusively to any entity whatsoever. Necessarily, nothing is both in motion and at rest.

Now the suggestion as to why we are dealing with a necessary predication here, is not quite the same as before. For it is not that the opposed predicate necessarily holds of a particular subject; but rather, that the two opposed predicates cannot both be said of a subject 'in every way'. But the basic idea is the same: once we have established that one of the two opposed predicates applied to something 'in every way', we have established that the other of the two opposed predicates may not be applied to it in any way.

What is wrong with the view that there is unlimited communion of Kinds, then, is that it allows all kinds of blatant self-contradiction. We *should* say that what is in motion is in no way at rest. But on the view that there is unlimited communion of Kinds, we could call anything by any name, and say that what is in motion is equally at rest, and *vice versa*. (The problem with the latelearners' view of the world, that Motion and Rest do not commune with Being, is rather more difficult and I shall not go into it here. It seems that if X does not commune with being, this implies the nonexistence of X – see 260ab).

I have argued that the idioms of essential and accidental predication are widely employed by Plato; but also, that the contrast between essential and accidental predication may be present, when the idioms are absent. It supports my construction of *Parmenides* 137 along these lines, that Plato makes the thinking I attribute to him there explicit in *Sophist* 245a. Similarly, the fact that Plato explicitly uses the notion of essential, as opposed to accidental, predication when talking of Forms in *Phaedo* 102-3 and *Republic* V, makes it easier to see the same ideas as underlying his treatment of the same topic in *Phaedo* 74 and *Protagoras* 330-1.

So let us now turn to examine these two passages.

The Disputed Passages

We may start our examination of these two passages by noting that the notions of identity and nonidentity are clearly rendered in both of them, by *tauton* (*Protagoras* 331b4), *ou tauton* (*Phaedo* 74c4) and *heteron* (*Phaedo* 74c7). Thus we may conclude that Plato knows that he is trying to prove the identity of justice with holiness in the *Protagoras*, and the non-identity of sensible equals with the Forms Equal in the *Phaedo*.

Another feature common to both passages is the use of the formula *toiouton einai hoion* ... (*Protagoras* 330c7, d5-6; *Phaedo* 74d7, 75b7). But this is not, in fact particularly significant. Taylor remarks that ' "such as to be F" is frequently used by Plato as equivalent to the simple "F" ' (p.113). And this point of view is borne out by a more detailed study of Plato's use of the formula where images are concerned, which has been carried out by Lee.[14] As Lee has pointed out, an image is said, in *Republic* X, to be τι τοιοῦτον οἷον τὸ ὄν, ὂν δε οὔ (597a4-5), and in *Sophist* 240a, a τι πρὸς τἀληθινὸν ἕτερον τοιοῦτον. Thus here the notion of being *toiouton hoion* is divorced from that of identity. But in the *Cratylus*, if an image has everything *toiouta hoiaper* X the model (434b7), then it is no longer an image of X, but another X. In the *Protagoras* too, to be *toiouton hoion* X is taken as evidence of identity with X, while in the *Phaedo*, particular equals are neither identical with the Form Equal, nor *toiouton hoion* it. Lee concludes that 'the word clearly carried all the slipperiness of the notion of image itself' (p.120, n.22).

But we can, perhaps, draw a slightly more determinate conclusion that this. An image may resemble what it is an image of, more, or less, closely. Now Plato is primarily interested in images that closely resemble what they are images of. Such images naturally share a great many of the attributes of their originals. But they do not, for Plato, share *all* the attributes with their originals, as the example of the two Cratyluses shows. For the two Cratyluses share all the same attributes (except their spatiotemporal location). They are two tokens of the same type, and the one is equally as real a Cratylus as is the other. For Plato, both are equally original Cratyluses, and neither is an image of Cratylus. We may conclude, then, that Plato looks for some difference in the attributes of the image and the original that is not just a difference in spatio-temporal location. A number of predicates apply both to the image and the original, in so far as the two are alike. But if the image is to be an image, rather than a second original, there must be some further predicate G, where G is not simply a matter of spatiotemporal location, such that the image is not-G, whereas the original is G.[15]

Thus we may say that in the *Protagoras*, the question under discussion is whether justice and holiness share the predicates that would render them identical; and in the *Phaedo* the question under discussion is whether the sensible equals and the Form Equal do or do not have some difference of attributes that renders them nonidentical.

Let us examine the *Protagoras* first then. In the *Protagoras*, Socrates is arguing for the unity of the virtues. At 330b6, he sets out on an argument about the relation of justice to holiness. Now in fact Socrates believes that justice is identical with holiness; and so we might expect him to argue, as C. C. W. Taylor point out (pp.108-9), that justice and holiness are alike in every respect. In fact, as Taylor (p.116) and Protagoras (331de) point out, Socrates' argument would at most show that justice and holiness are not altogether unlike one another. But, that apart, the argument also contains a logical error that Taylor notes, but Protagoras passes by. Now Taylor gives a reconstruction of Socrates' argument that exploits the notion of essential predication (p.116). So let us focus our attention on the logical error as it figures in this version of the argument.

The argument would then require us to proceed from Taylor's 9a:

It is not an essential feature of holiness that it is just, to Taylor's 12a:

It is a feature of holiness that it is not just.

As Taylor points out, what is wrong with this argument is that 'though being just cannot be an essential feature of holiness, it might be a non-essential feature' (p.116).

But against the background I have sketched out of Plato's subsequent interest in essential predication, we can, I believe, reconstruct a more plausible line of thought. We have seen that a property F may belong to a particular x either 'in some way', or 'in every way', and that essential predications assume the second of these two forms. And if a property does belong to something 'in every way', then the opposed property does not belong to it 'in any way'. So the idea there would be, that 'just' might be said of holiness either 'in some way' or 'in every way'; if 'just' is essentially predicated of holiness, then 'unjust' is not true of it 'in any way'. If, however, 'just' is only accidentally predicated of holiness, then 'not just' as well as 'just' will be true of it. In other words, if it is not an essential feature of holiness that it is just, then it is a feature of holiness that it is not just.

Now it might be objected that this is an unduly subtle reading of the Greek text here. After all, Taylor's 9a represents 331a7-8, which reads simply: Οὐκ ἄρα ἐστὶν ὁσιότης οἶον δίκαιον εἶναι πρᾶγμα and his 12a represents 331a9, which runs: ἡ δ᾽ ὁσιότης οἶον μὴ δίκαιον. On any reading, though, this passage looks forward to later developments in Plato's thought. It marks the earliest appearance of the self-predication assumption, which is subsequently to be associated with the theory of Forms. It is fair enough, then, in these circumstances, to see the passage in the light of Plato's later doctrines. And my contention is that the reading I have offered of the passage indicates how Plato would have developed the same line of thought, had he written this passage later in his career.

Let us turn now to *Phaedo* 74-5. It is not, I believe, possible to demonstrate conclusively that this passage exploits a distinction between essential and accidental predication, and does not reveal a confusion between identity and predication. All I hope to show, in fact, is that such a reading of the passage is possible and that there is not an overwhelming case against it.

The opening move in the argument here has provoked much controversy. In 74c1-2, Socrates poses the two questions: αὐτὰ τὰ ἴσα ἔστιν ὅτε ἄνισα σοι ἐφάνη, ἤ ἡ ἰσότης ἀνισότης; The issue here is whether or not the two questions are identical. Certainly, both questions expect the same answer ('yes'), but does Plato regard them as equivalent, as simply two ways of asking the same thing? It is often thought that if Plato does regard them as equivalent, then he must be confused between identity and predication. After all, the first question has a predicative form, whereas the second question has the form of an identity judgement.

This conclusion does not, however, follow inevitably. For suppose that the particular equals, the sticks and stones, are equal only accidentally, while the Form Equal is 'in every way', or essentially, equal. The particular equals will then be both equal and unequal; but the Form equal will be just equal (and the Form Unequal, we will suppose, just unequal). In this case, the Form Equal would never seem unequal, nor yet would it ever seem to be the Form Unequal. If things were otherwise, then 'equal' and 'unequal' could be predicated of the Forms Equal and Unequal alike; but if that were so, then the Form Equal could be confused with the Form Unequal (and *vice versa*). For there would then be no way of telling these two Forms apart. (We make here the further supposition that these two Forms have no other distinctive properties. But this seems in line with Platonic doctrine.) So if we can appeal to essential predication here, we can read the two questions in such a way that they do indeed put one and the same point in different ways; but we need not thereby attribute to Plato a confusion between identity and predication. We do in fact find here, with *estin hote*, a temporal qualification in play in the question.

The point is, that the equals themselves *never* seem unequal: they are essentially equal. And this is the reason why equality never seems to be inequality. It is, as we have seen, a central feature of the theory of Forms that the Form F is essentially F; and it is reasonable to suppose that it is to this that Plato is appealing here when he contrasts the Form Equal with the sensible particular equals that are both equal and unequal.

Another passage in the argument here also deserves brief comment. In 74d5-7, Socrates asks ἆρα φαίνεται ἡμῖν οὕτως ἴσα εἶναι ὥσπερ αὐτὸ τὸ ὅ ἔστιν, ἢ ἐνδεῖ τι ἐκείνου τῷ τοιοῦτον εἶναι οἷον τὸ ἴσον, ἢ οὐδέν; now clearly this question calls for a contrast between two modes of being equal. Gallop in his commentary suggests that the contrast is that sensible equals are equal in the predicative sense, but that the Form Equal is equal, because it is identical with equal (pp.127-8). There are two problems with Gallop's view however. One is that all sensible equals alike fail in this regard (75b7), and that it is scarcely plausible to regard them all as striving after identity with the Form Equal. The other is that to be identical with the Form Equal is not, of course, to be equal, in any real sense. A difference between two modes of being equal is at least as well satisfied by a distinction between being essentially and being accidentally equal. And as Plato certainly thinks that these modes of being do typify Forms and particulars, it is reasonable to suppose that he may have it in mind here.

Conclusion

We have seen (in chapter 4 above) that a theory of paradigmatic Forms may be required in Plato's theory of explanation, and of Forms as explanations. We have seen too (in chapters 2 and 3) how a theory of paradigmatic Forms is the natural consequence of Plato's view of contradiction. Plato needs a theory of entities that are (F) and are not (not-F) at all times and in all contexts. In this chapter, we have seen how this need issues in a theory of essential predication (the Form F is, as opposed to particular F's, 'in every way' or 'at all times' F). More generally, we have seen that many of Plato's (otherwise puzzling) claims about Forms can be understood on the hypothesis that Plato is primarily interested in safeguarding Forms from any suggestion of real or apparent contradiction; and that we need not resort to attributing to Plato a confusion between identity and predication.

1. Except, as Rohr points out (281) stars; and particular stars, unlike the Form Star, change their position.

2. See Taylor, Plato's '*Protagoras*' 112; Gallop, Plato's '*Phaedo*' 125; Owen, 'Notes on Ryle's Plato' 349, 355.

3. On Parmenides' use of *einai*, see Kirk and Raven, *The Presocratic Philosophers* 269-272; Owen 'Eleatic Questions'; Furth 'Elements of Eleatic Ontology'.

4. For one example of this view, see Gosling, *Plato* 193.

5. See Gallop 193. Gallop reiterates this point in his 'Relations in the *Phaedo*' 155.

6. Hackforth 155. Hackforth also claims here that the threefold distinction would be 'irrelevant to his immediate purposes and to the whole final argument for immortality'.

7. O'Brien, 'The Last Argument of Plato's *Phaedo*' 199-200, esp. 200 n.2. F. C. White, 'Particulars in *Phaedo* 95e-107a', also appreciates the contrast drawn here between essential and accidental predication; but makes no reference to the important linguistic markers.

8. See Frede 35 for a discussion of questions of this form.

9. Thus Robinson is able to believe that in the *Parmenides* and in the *Sophist*, Plato sometimes distinguishes identity from predication, but at other times sets before us arguments that fallaciously overlook this distinction (*Plato's Earlier Dialectic* 252).

10. In English, of course, propositions of the form 'the S is S' look to be predications, and not identities. While the same word may indeed stand on both sides of the verb, the same expression does not. As against this, it might be argued that Plato wrote Greek and not English. But for an example of an identity statement in Greek where Plato does insert the definite article on both sides of the equation, see *Parmenides* 157b9.

Frede (68) suggests that propositions of this form are not identity statements, but examples of the first of the two uses of '... is ...' which he finds in the *Sophist*. For comment on Frede's view of the *Sophist*, see my 'Plato's Task in the *Sophist*' (forthcoming).

A further complication is that Plato sometimes seems to take the expression 'the S' as 'the things that are S', and sometimes as 'the property of being S'. But this complication seems irrelevant to the matter in hand.

11. This sort of analysis is also offered by Nehamas. See his 'Predication and Forms of Opposites in the *Phaedo*' 475.

12. Similar propositions to that in 137d3 are to be found at 138b4-5, 138c2, and 140c9-d2 in the first movement, and at 149a1-2 in the second.

13. Frede reaches this conclusion despite – or perhaps because of – linking this passage with *Sophist* 255-6.

14. See 'The Second Third Man: An Interpretation'.

15. I here follow Vlastos, 'Degrees of Reality' 60-63.

CONCLUSION

We have now answered the questions we set ourselves in chapter 1 of this work. We have seen both why Plato felt the need to posit Forms, thus departing from the ontology of the Socratic dialogues, and why it is that Forms have the character that they do. Plato, I have suggested, misunderstood the relation of context to contradiction; and that is why Plato posits Forms, but other philosophers do not.

But we are still, not surprisingly, far from a full understanding of the theory of Forms. Our explanation of why Plato had a theory of Forms has not gone far towards accounting for either the philosophical depth or the continuing philosophical interest of the theory of Forms. These omissions will not be made good in this conclusion. But perhaps a few brief historical remarks will be in order. Certainly it is an important fact about Plato's theory of Forms that it forms part of a philosophical tradition reaching at least from Parmenides to Aristotle; and we should take some account of this in our final assessment of the theory.

We have seen how, in his middle period, Plato thinks that there must be Forms, if there is to be knowledge, or satisfactory explanation. He remarks, after criticizing the theory in the *Parmenides*, that if the theory isn't true, there will be nothing to turn one's thought towards, and no possibility of conversation (135b5-c1). On the interpretation I have advanced, this will be because of the numerous apparent contradictions that would then face us, for which we would lack a satisfactory resolution. The same two concerns (with the possibility of language, and the fear of contradiction) are, of course, coupled by Aristotle in his defence of the law of contradiction (an opponent of the law must first speak, and then his word must be meaningful, if he is to be refuted). The idea that there is a link here is clearly inherited ultimately from Parmenides. The possibility of conversation is perhaps alien to the Eleatic world-view; yet Parmenides clearly has a concern for the possibility of thought (internal conversation). Parmenides clearly believes that we don't think, although we could. He thinks we make two basic errors – that of talking of notbeing, which is unintelligible, and that of mingling such talk with talk of being, thus contradicting ourselves. For Parmenides, the only true reference for thought is the intelligible, and uncontradictory, Eleatic One.

Now in fact the most powerful attack on Parmenides in antiquity is launched by Plato in his *Sophist*. Plato argues there that what is notbeing can indeed, as mortals always assume, coincide with what is being; and that once we acknowledge this, there is no longer a problem of the unintelligibility of notbeing. It is a measure of the power of Parmenides' original thought, however, that while Aristotle in *Metaphysics E* praises Plato for his work in the *Sophist* in assigning sophistry to what is notbeing (on the grounds that sophists deal in the coincidental, and the coincidental is close to the notbeing), he declines to recognize a *theoria* of the coincidental (or, that is, the notbeing). He agrees with Parmenides that here is no route of enquiry; and, like the Plato of the middle period, is interested in transforming rather than rejecting, the thought of his Eleatic predecessors.

The second point of inheritance we should note in this tradition concerns the relation of epistemology to metaphysics. Parmenides' view of what there is, is a view of what there must be; and his view of what there must be derives from a consideration of the nature of human thought. Parmenides' metaphysics is posterior to his epistemology. We have seen that the same is true for Plato: in chapters 3 and 4, we have seen Plato argue that we can know the world, and explain the things that are in it: so there must be Forms. Aristotle too argues from epistemology to metaphysics. Aristotle in fact thinks we can know the world without the mediation of Forms. But for Aristotle, like his predecessors, the world is, as it must be, if we are to know it. The various forms of coincidence (for most of us, real enough), are not such as to be known; and they do not form a significant part of the world.

We see from Parmenides to Aristotle *via* Plato a clear line of descent; and we also gain a clear sense of progress. Aristotle's views are very persuasive, whereas no-one today (or indeed ever) would believe Parmenides.

Now I have concentrated on that aspect of Plato's response to Parmenides that now seems to us to be mistaken, and about which Plato himself changes his mind in the *Sophist* – that is, Plato's mistaken belief that being cannot be combined with notbeing in one and the same entity without contradiction. But it is appropriate here to note the high degree of philosophical inventiveness displayed by Plato's response to Parmenides, taken as a whole. Parmenides poses for Plato the question 'is the world really contradictory and unknowable?' – to which Plato returns the answer 'no: only it cannot be known or explained without reference to Forms'. Parmenides' views on thought and knowledge were not to be discarded, nor was his view as to the primacy of epistemology over metaphysics. At the same time, Plato recognizes that we live in the real, and not the Eleatic universe; and gives an account of how we can know, and understand, our actual environment. All this is achieved by the simple hypothesis that there are Forms. Of Forms we have immediate knowledge, and of the sensible world we have knowledge mediated through Forms.

Plato may not have made the right response here to Parmenides; but he has made a great advance on his greatest philosophical predecessor. And there is all we can ask of any philosopher.

BIBLIOGRAPHY

Allen, R. E., *Plato's Euthyphro and the Earlier Theory of Forms* (London 1970).

Anderson, J., 'The Problem of Causality', *Australasian Journal of Psychology and Philosophy* 16 (1938) 127-142.

Annas, J., *Aristotle's Metaphysics Books M and N*, translated with Introduction and Notes (Oxford 1976).

Annas, J., 'Forms and First Principles', *Phronesis* 19 (1974) 257-283.

Bolton, R., 'Plato's Distinction between Being and Becoming' RM 29 (1975) 66-95.

Brentlinger, J. A. 'Incomplete Predicates and the Two-World Theory of the *Phaedo*', *Phronesis* 17 (1972) 51-79.

Burge, E. L., 'The Ideas as *Aitiai* in the *Phaedo*', *Phronesis* 16 (1971) 1-13.

Burnet, J. *Plato's Phaedo* (Oxford 1911).

Burnyeat, M. F., 'Aristotle on Understanding Knowledge', in *Aristotle On Science: The Posterior Analytics*, ed. E. Berti (Padua 1981) 97-139.

Cherniss, H. F., 'The Philosophical Economy of the Theory of Ideas', *AJPh* 56 (1936) 445-456*.

Cherniss, H. F., 'The Relation of the *Timaeus* to Plato's Later Dialogues', *AJPh* 78 (1957) 225-266*.

Crombie, I. M., *An Examination of Plato's Doctrines* 2 vols (vol. I London 1962; vol. II London 1963).

Cross, R. C. 'Logos and Forms in Plato', *Mind* 63 (1954) 433-50*.

Cross, R. C. and Woozley, A. D., *Plato's Republic* (London 1964).

Davidson, D. 'How is Weakness of the Will Possible?, in *Moral Concepts*, ed. J. Feinberg (Oxford 1969) 93-113.

Evans, J. D. G., *Aristotle's Concept Of Dialectic* (Cambridge 1977)

Fine, G., 'Knowledge and Belief in *Republic* V', *AGPh* 60 (1978) 121-139.

Fine, G., 'The One over Many', *PR* 89 (1980) 197-240.

Furth, M., 'Elements of Eleatic Ontology', *Journal Of The History Of Philosophy* 6 (1968) 111-132, reprinted in *The Presocratics* ed. A. P. D. Mourelatos (New York 1974) 241-270.

Gallop, D., 'Plato on Relations', *Canadian Journal Of Philosophy* Supp. Vol. 2 (1976).

Gallop, D., *Plato's Phaedo*, translated with Notes (Oxford 1975).

Gosling, J. C. B. '*Doxa* and *Dynamis* in Plato's *Republic*', *Phronesis* 13 (1968) 119-130.

Gosling, J. C. B. *Plato* (London 1973).

Gosling, J. C. B. '*Republic* Book 5: *Ta Polla Kala* etc.', *Phronesis* 5 (1960) 116-128.

Hackforth, R., *Plato's Phaedo* (Cambridge 1955).

Hardie, R. F., *A Study In Plato* (Oxford 1936).

Hare, R. M., 'Plato and the Mathematicians', in *New Studies In Plato And Aristotle*, ed. R. Bambrough (London 1965) 21-38.

Hicken, W. F., 'Knowledge and Forms in Plato's *Theaetetus*', *JHS* 77 (1957) 48-53*.

Hintikka, J. J. K., *Time and Necessity* (Oxford 1973).

Hodges, W., *Logic* (Harmondsworth 1977).

Irwin, T. H. 'Plato's Heracliteanism', *PQ* 27 (1977) 1-12.

Irwin, T. H., *Plato's Moral Theory* (Oxford 1977).

Kahn, C. H., 'Some Philosophical Uses of "To Be' in Plato', *Phronesis* 26 (1981) 105-134.

Kirk, G. S. and Raven, J. E., *The Presocratic Philosophers* (Cambridge 1957).

Kirwan, C., 'Plato and Relativity', *Phronesis* 19 (1974) 112-129.

Lee, E. N., 'The Second Third Man: an Interpretation', in *Patterns In Plato's Thought*, Papers Arising out of the West Coast Greek Philosophy Conference, ed. J. M. E. Moravcsik (Dordecht/Boston 1973) 101-122.

Loriaux, R., *Le Phédon de Plato* (Namur 1969).

Macdowell, J., *Plato's Theaetetus*, translated with Notes (Oxford 1973).

Mackie, J. L., 'Causes and Conditions', *APhQ* 2 (1965) 245-264, reprinted in *Causes and Conditionals*, ed. E. Sosa (Oxford 1975) 15-38.

Mackie, J. L. *The Cement of the Universe* (Oxford 1974).

Moore, G. E., *Some Main Problems of Philosophy* (London 1953).

Moravcsik, J. M. E., 'Recollecting the Theory of Forms' in *Facets Of Plato's Philosophy*, ed. W. H. Werkmeister, *Phronesis* Supp. Vol. II (Assen 1976) 1-20.

Murphy, N., *Plato's Republic* (Oxford 1951).

Nehamas, A., 'Plato on the Imperfection of the Sensible World' *APhQ* (1975) 105-117.

Nehamas, A., 'Predication and Forms of Opposites in Plato's *Phaedo*', *RM* 26 (1973) 461-491.

O'Brien, D., 'The Last Argument of Plato's *Phaedo*', *CQ* n.s. 17 (1967) 198-231 and *CQ* n.s. 18 (1968) 95-106.

Owen, G. E. L., 'Eleatic Questions', *CQ* n.s. 10 (1960) 84-102.

Owen, G. E. L., 'Notes on Ryle's Plato', in *Ryle*, ed. O. P. Wood, and G. Pitcher (London 1971) 341-372.

Owen, G. E. L., 'Plato on Notbeing', in *Plato* vol. I, ed. G. Vlastos (London 1972) 223-267.

Owen, G. E. L., 'A Proof in the *Peri Ideon*', *JHS* 77 (1957) 103-111.

Prauss, G., *Platon und der logische Eleatismus* (Berlin 1966).

Quine, W. V. O., 'Quantifiers and Propositional Attitudes', *JPhil* 53 (1956) 177-187, reprinted in *Reference And Modality*, ed. L. Linsky (Oxford 1971) 101-111.

Robinson, R., 'Forms and Error in Plato's *Theaetetus*', *PR* 59 (1950) 3-30.

Robinson, R., 'Plato's Separation of Reason from Desire', *Phronesis* 16 (1971) 38-48.

Robinson, R., *Plato's Earlier Dialectic*, 2nd ed. (Oxford 1953).

Rohr, D., 'Plato on Empty Forms', *AGPh* 60 (1978) 268-283.

Ross, W. D., *Aristotle's Metaphysics*, A revised text with Introduction and Commentary (Oxford 1924).

Russell, B., *An Introduction to Mathematical Philosophy* (London 1919).

Russell, B., *The Problems of Philosophy* (Oxford 1912).

Ryle, G., 'Plato's *Parmenides*', *Mind* 48 (1939) 129-151, 302-325.

Schiebe, E., 'Über Relativbegriffe in der Philosophie Platons' *Phronesis* 12 (1967) 28-49.

Stenzel, J., *Plato's Method of Dialectic*, translated by D. J. Allen (Oxford 1940).

Stough, C., 'Forms and Explanation in the *Phaedo*', *Phronesis* 21 (1977) 1-30.

Strang, C., 'Plato and the Third Man', *PASS* 37 (1963) 147-163; reprinted in *Plato* vol. I, ed. G. Vlastos (London 1972) 184-200.

Taylor, C. C. W., 'Forms as Causes in the *Phaedo*' *Mind* 78 (1969) 45-59.

Taylor, C. C. W., *Plato's Protagoras* (Oxford 1976).

Van Fraasen, B. C., 'The Pragmatics of Explanation', *APhQ* 14 (1977) 143-150.

Vlastos, G., 'Degrees of Reality in Plato', in *New Studies In Plato And Aristotle*, ed. R. Bambrough (London 1965) 1-19, reprinted in *Platonic Studies* 58-75.

Vlastos, G., 'A Metaphysical Paradox', *Proceedings Of The American Philosophical Association* 39 (1966) 5-19; reprinted in *Platonic Studies* 38-57.

Vlastos, G., 'Reasons and Causes in the *Phaedo*' in *Plato*, vol. I, ed. G. Vlastos (London 1972); reprinted in *Platonic Studies* 43-57.

White, F. C., 'J. Gosling on *Ta Polla Kala*', *Phronesis* 23 (1978) 127-131.

White, F. C., 'The Compresence of Opposites in *Phaedo* 102', *CQ* n.s. 27 (1977) 303-311.

White, F. C., 'Particulars in *Phaedo* 95e-107a', *Canadian Journal Of Philosophy* Supp. Vol. 2 (1976) 129-147.

White, F. C., 'Plato's Middle Dialogues and the Independence of Particulars' *PQ* 27 (1977) 193-213.

White, F. C., 'The *Phaedo* and *Republic* V on Essences', *JHS* 98 (1978) 142-156.

---

*reprinted in *Studies In Plato's Metaphysics* ed. by R. E. Allen (London, 1965)

INDEX